MW01152484

Korean Grammar with Cat Memes

First Edition: October 2017

ISBN. 978-1978091627

www.easy-korean.com

Contents

Preface

Learning a foreign language is never easy. You have to memorize many words and learn the rules of the language, which is known as grammar. Korean grammar, in particular, is notorious for being too difficult for many people. That is why Korean Grammar with Cat Memes was created. This book breaks down the basic concepts of the Korean language in the easiest way possible.

Hangul or No Hangul? You Decide!

Most Korean classes begin with Hangul, the Korean alphabet. Instead of focusing on listening and speaking for beginners, many instructors emphasize learning Hangul first. However, Hangul is a writing system and is mainly for reading and writing. Think of a baby learning his first language. By the time he learns the alphabet, he is already speaking fluently. Learning Hangul, therefore, is optional.

At the same time, Hangul is quite easy to learn. In fact, that is exactly why King Sejong created it. Hangul makes reading and writing super easy. So you have two options. You can either learn Hangul first or you can skip the first three chapters of this book and start learning Korean grammar immediately. Every Korean sentence is written in Hangul and English. Here is a preview.

친구랑 같이 왔어요. = I came here with my friend.

(Cheen-goo-rahng gah-chee wah-ssuh-yoh.)

If you prefer reading Korean sentences in Hangul, start with Chapter 1. If not, you can go to Chapter 4 directly. Remember, you can choose to learn Hangul at any time.

How to Study Korean as a Beginner

To learn to speak, you have to do the exact opposite. You have to listen and listen a lot. Listening is how people learn to speak any language (well, except sign languages). So find yourself a few different sources of listening content. This book won't be nearly as effective if your ears are not exposed to spoken Korean. In other words, books are not enough. Try to listen to people speak Korean even though you may not understand them. It could be the difference between learning Korean or not. Fortunately, many Korean dramas, TV shows, and movies are available digitally. EASY KOREAN also provides free listening content on YouTube. But listening won't be too much fun if you don't know any words in Korean. Ideally, a beginner should memorize at least 500 to 1,000 words. (Purchase the Korean Words with Cat Memes books on major online bookstores and get the most essential Korean words for beginners.)

Cat Memes! Because Why Not?

To make studying more fun, a cat meme is included in every chapter. The memes show photos of two house cats, Soomba and Zorro. In case anyone is curious, here is a little bit of information on who they are.

Soomba (숨바꼭질)

Female

Loves tuna and chicken

Knows how to control her owner

Zorro (조로)

Male

Loves special treats

Toilet-trained, can open doors

1. Hangul Vowels

Hangul, the Korean writing system, was invented by King Sejong and his men during the 1400s. Without it, people had to memorize thousands of Chinese characters for reading and writing. So it is not a surprise that many Koreans are very grateful for this invention. Hangul makes reading and writing Korean so much easier.

한글

This is the word 'Hangul' written in Hangul. (You can also spell it as 'Hangeul.') Just like the English alphabet, Hangul has consonant and vowel parts. Let's first discuss the vowels. Here are ten basic vowel shapes of Hangul.

ㅣ ㅏ ㅑ ㅓ ㅕ

ㅡ ㅗ ㅛ ㅜ ㅠ

Notice how the first set has long vertical lines and the second set is made up of long horizontal lines. The vertical ones are placed on the right side of consonant letters. The horizontal shapes are placed at the bottom of consonants. (We will discuss more about this in the next chapter.)

ㅣ

This letter is called 이 (ee). It sounds exactly like its name, "ee." Every Hangul vowel sounds like its name. But what about the circle shape on the left?

A complete Hangul character is made up of at least one consonant and one vowel. That is why vowels are sometimes written with the consonant ㅇ (ee-eung). This O-shaped letter acts as a space filler and does not change the sound of the vowel.

ㅇ (no sound) + ㅣ (ee) = 이 (ee)

So ㅣ (ee) and 이 (ee) can be considered the same except 이 (ee) is a complete character where ㅣ (ee) is just a vowel letter.

ㅏ

This is 아 (ah). What does this vowel sound like? "Ah."

ㅑ

This is 야 (yah).

ㅓ

This is 어 (uh).

ㅕ

This is 여 (yuh).

There are more vowel letters with long vertical lines, but let's look at some of the horizontal shapes.

—

This is 으 (eu). (It sounds like "brrrrr" without the consonant sounds in the beginning.)

ㅗ

This is 오 (oh).

ㅛ

This is **요** (yoh).

ㅜ

This is **우** (woo).

ㅠ

This is **유** (you).

Now how about some practice? We can apply what we've covered so far with English consonants.

D ㅏ RT

Can you guess what this "word" might sound like? The vowel here is **아** (ah). So it sounds like "dart."

D ㅓ RT

This one has the vowel ㅓ (uh). So the word would sound like "dirt."

B ㅓ RD

This one sounds like "bird."

B

ㅗ

This one contains ㅗ (oh), so it sounds like "boh." Notice how this vowel shape is placed below B.

B

ㅜ

This sounds like "boo."

Now what about the following?

B | B | D |

B ㅏ B | D |

B

ㅜ

What would these six characters sound like? The answer is "bibbidi-bobbidi-boo," just like the song. We will discuss consonant shapes of Hangul in the next chapter, but let's look at a few more vowel shapes before we move on.

ㅔ

This is 에 (eh).

ㅐ

This is 애 (ae). Think of ㅔ (eh) as 'e' in 'then' whereas ㅐ (ae) is 'a' in 'than.'

ㅘ

This is 와 (wah). Interestingly, this letter is a combination of ㅗ (oh) and ㅏ (ah). But it still represents a single syllable. 와 (wah) sounds like pronouncing "oh" and "ah" really quickly.

ㅝ

This is 워 (wuh).

ㅚ

This is 외 (weh).

ㅟ

This is 위 (wee).

ㅢ

This is 의 (eui). For many people, this pronunciation seems difficult at first. Basically, ㅢ (eui) is combining ㅡ (eu) and ㅣ (ee) together. It sounds somewhat like "eu-ee" spoken really quickly.

Can you guess what the following words say?

BㅐN

BㅔN

Which one says "ben?" What about "ban?" The first word looks like 'B-A-N.' The second one says 'B-E-N.'

ㅘ

ㅝ

ㅚ

ㅟ

What are the names of these four shapes? From the top, they are 와 (wah), 워 (wuh), 외 (weh), and 위 (wee).

Lastly, here are the rest of the vowel letters. These Hangul shapes are not as common, but you might still see them from time to time.

ㅒ

This is 얘 (yaeh).

ㅖ

This is 예 (yeah).

ㅙ

This is 왜 (wae).

ㅞ

This is 웨 (weah).

Congratulations! You are now almost ready to read words in Hangul. (We will go through the consonant letters in the next chapter.)

2. Hangul Consonants

Here are ten consonant letters of 한글 (hahn-geul).

ㄱ ㄷ ㅂ ㅅ ㅈ

ㄲ ㄸ ㅃ ㅆ ㅉ

The first one is ㄱ (geu). It is also known as 기역 (ghee-yuhg). Unlike vowels, consonant parts have unique names. However, the names are not as important as what they sound like. So let's just focus on their pronunciations.

ㄱ

Again, this is ㄱ (geu). This letter is similar to G. If the vowel ㅏ (ah) is added, it looks like the following.

ㄱ (geu) + ㅏ (ah) = 가 (gah)

By the way, main consonants are always written first. Then vowels are written on the right side or below the consonants.

ㄲ

This is ㄲ (ggeu). This letter is a double consonant, which is basically ㄱ (geu) written twice. There are five double consonant shapes in Hangul. They sound much stronger and more abrupt than the single counterparts.

ㄷ

This is ㄷ (deu). It is similar to D. For example, ㄷ (deu) and ㅏ (ah) will form 다 (dah).

ㄸ

This is the double form of ㄷ (deu). We can call it ㄸ (ddeu). (To pronounce this letter, hold the ㄷ (deu) sound with your tongue placed on top of your mouth before releasing it in a burst.)

ㅂ

This is ㅂ (beu), like the letter B.

ㅃ

The double ㅂ (beu) is ㅃ (bbeu).

ㅅ

ㅅ (seu) is like the letter S spoken very softly. It is similar to the final sound of "bananas."

ㅆ

Double ㅅ (seu) is ㅆ (sseu). This letter sounds much more like S.

ㅈ

This is ㅈ (jeu), like the letter J.

ㅉ

The double form of ㅈ (jeu) is ㅉ (jjeu).

We can now add the vowel ㅗ (oh) to these consonants to form complete characters.

고 도 보 소 조

꼬 또 뽀 쏘 쪼

The first line says "goh doh boh soh joh." The second line sounds like "ggoh ddoh bboh ssoh jjoh." (Imagine a young child speaking with a tiny mouth.)

Here are the rest of the consonants.

ㄴ ㄹ ㅁ ㅊ

ㅋ ㅌ ㅍ ㅎ

We've already discussed ㅇ (eu) in the previous chapter, so we can skip it. Unlike the first ten consonants like ㄱ (geu) and ㄷ (deu), these eight letters do not have double forms.

ㄴ

This is ㄴ (neu). 내, ㄴ + ㅐ, sounds like "nae."

ㄹ

This is ㄹ (reu). The letter's sound is similar to L and R but not quite the same. Depending on the situation, ㄹ (reu) can sound closer to L or R. For instance, 루, ㄹ + ㅜ, can be written in English as either 'loo' or 'roo.'

ㅁ

This is ㅁ (meu). 머, ㅁ + ㅓ, sounds like "muh."

ㅊ

This is ㅊ (cheu). 치, ㅊ + ㅣ, sounds like "chee."

ㅋ

This is ㅋ (keu). 카, ㅋ + ㅏ, sounds like "kah."

ㅌ

This is ㅌ (teu). 터, ㅌ + ㅓ, sounds like "tuh."

ㅍ

This is ㅍ (peu). 페, ㅍ + ㅔ, sounds like "peh."

ㅎ

This is ㅎ (heu). 호, ㅎ + ㅗ, sounds like "hoh."

In the next and final chapter of Hangul, we will put consonants and vowels together to form actual words.

3. Hangul Exercises

Let's do a quick review of all the vowel and consonant shapes from the previous chapters. First, let's look at the vowel letters.

ㅣ ㅏ ㅑ ㅓ ㅕ ㅡ ㅗ ㅛ ㅜ ㅠ

ㅔ ㅐ ㅘ ㅝ ㅚ ㅟ ㅢ ㅒ ㅖ ㅙ ㅞ

Try to memorize at least the first line if you can. Unlike English, a Hangul character does not put two or more vowels next to each other. For instance, writing 'Asia' in Hangul would require three separate characters.

아 시 아

A si a

By the way, 'Asia' is pronounced "ah-shee-ah" in Korean.

Now let's review all the consonant letters.

ㄱ ㄲ ㄷ ㄸ ㅂ ㅃ ㅅ ㅆ ㅈ ㅉ

ㄴ ㄹ ㅁ ㅇ ㅊ ㅋ ㅌ ㅍ ㅎ

A Hangul character not only has a main consonant, but it may also have a base consonant known as 받침 (baht-cheem). Let's look at the following two words to see how base consonants work.

바치 (bah-chee)

받침 (baht-cheem)

The first word has only one consonant letter per character. However, the second word has two consonants each; one main consonant and one base consonant. Characters can have up to two base consonants.

값 (gahb)

This character has ㄱ (geu) as the main consonant and ㅂ (beu) and ㅅ (seu) as the base consonants. In case there are two base consonants, only one of them is pronounced. Here is the order of pronunciation for this word.

1. ㄱ (geu)

2. ㅏ (ah)

3. ㅂ (beu) or ㅅ (seu)

The main consonant is pronounced first, followed by the vowel, and then one of the base consonants. For this particular word, ㅅ (seu) is silent. That means ㅂ (beu) must be pronounced.

$$ㄱ + ㅏ + ㅂㅅ$$

(geu + ah + beu)

So 값 sounds like "gahb."

A character with no base consonant finishes with a vowel and will have an open sound. If it contains at least one base consonant, then it will have a closed sound.

Ending with a vowel: 코 (koh)

Ending with a consonant: 콘 (kohn)

When consonant letters are used as base consonants, they may have different pronunciations. Let's take a look at characters where the main and base consonants are the same. We will use ㅜ (woo) as the vowel.

국 (goog)

눈 (noon)

둗 (doot)

룰 (rool)

뭄 (moom)

붑 (boob)

숫 (soot)

웅 (woong)

줏 (joot)

춫 (choot)

쿡 (kook)

툳 (toot)

풒 (poop)

훝 (hoot)

숫 (soot), for example, has ㅅ (seu) as the main consonant and base consonant. But it sounds like "soot" and not "soos." (This may seem confusing at first, but you will get used to it with enough practice.)

Let's look at how English-based words are written in Hangul. These words may have different meanings in Korean as they have become part of the Korean language over the years.

가스 (gah-sseu) = gas

빌딩 (beel-ding) = building

콜라 (cohl-lah) = coke (soft drink)

사이다 (sah-ee-dah) = clear soft drink like Sprite

아파트 (ah-pah-teu) = apartment

디씨 (dee-ssee) = discount (d/c)

리모콘 (ree-moh-cohn) = remote control

파이팅 (pah-ee-ting) = fighting

Fighting? What does it mean in Korean? **파이팅** (pah-ee-ting) is basically a chant. It means 'go get 'em,' 'good luck,' or 'break a leg.'

We are finally done with learning Hangul for now. Remember that this book does not require you to read Hangul at all. You can read every Korean word or sentence in this book in English, which is okay for beginners. Learn to speak first. You can always read and write later.

4. Korean Grammar

Many people say Korean grammar is the hardest. Well, that may not be true at all. People in Korea have no problem understanding Korean and most of them have never read a book about it. As long as you are exposed to the language, your brain will naturally figure out what the rules are. But you can also take a shortcut and save time by reading about the rules.

This book presents the basic rules of speaking Korean. Each grammar chapter is based on questions and answers. However, you don't necessarily have to memorize the rules. In fact, grammar is all about understanding and being aware of what the rules are. Once you finish this book, try to listen to Korean and memorize Korean words as much as possible. Then you should be able to speak Korean in no time.

5. How to Say Hello

Q. How do people say hello in Korean?

Most people would tell you that you say **안녕하세요** (ahn-nyuhng-hah-seh-yoh) to say hello in Korean. But that is not entirely accurate. Think of different ways of saying hello in English. People don't always use the word 'hello' to greet someone. Korean works the same way. If you've watched Korean dramas, you may have noticed how the characters almost never say **안녕하세요** (ahn-nyuhng-hah-seh-yoh) to each other.

Q. Then when should I use 안녕하세요 (ahn-nyuhng-hah-seh-yoh)?

안녕하세요 (ahn-nyuhng-hah-seh-yoh) is something you can say when you meet a person for the first time. It is a formal greeting between two people that are not familiar with one another. That is why you would never say **안녕하세요** (ahn-nyuhng-hah-seh-yoh) to your mother, unless you are drunk. Interestingly, you can still use this phrase toward your teachers even though you may have known them for years. How come? Well, the relationship between a teacher and student is considered more formal than informal.

Here is one more thing about **안녕하세요** (ahn-nyuhng-hah-seh-yoh). Even though it is written as **요** (yoh) at the end, it is usually pronounced "**여** (yuh)." It is only because **여** (yuh) is a little easier to pronounce than **요** (yoh). Also, Korean is usually spoken without intonation or stress. So **안녕하세요** (ahn-nyuhng-hah-seh-yoh) would be spoken in a flat manner unlike how the word 'hello' is spoken in English.

Q. What is 안녕 (ahn-nyuhng) and how is it different from 안녕하세요 (ahn-nyuhng-hah-seh-yoh)?

안녕 (ahn-nyuhng) is the short version of 안녕하세요 (ahn-nyuhng-hah-seh-yoh). This is how people greet their friends. For greeting someone much older, you would have to use 안녕하세요 (ahn-nyuhng-hah-seh-yoh) and never 안녕 (ahn-nyuhng). We will discuss this topic more in the next chapter.

One major difference between 안녕 (ahn-nyuhng) and 안녕하세요 (ahn-nyuhng-hah-seh-yoh) is that 안녕 (ahn-nyuhng) can either mean 'hello' or 'good-bye.' On the other hand, 안녕하세요 (ahn-nyuhng-hah-seh-yoh) is only used to say hello.

Q. So what is another way of saying hello in Korean?

Korean speakers would often say 왔어? (wah-ssuh?) or 오셨어요? (oh-shuh-ssuh-yoh?) when they see someone arriving. Both expressions mean 'You're here?' or 'You've arrived?'

왔어? (wah-ssuh?) is used toward friends and siblings. On the other hand, 오셨어요? (oh-shuh-ssuh-yoh?) is used toward others, especially people who are much older than the speaker.

6. JDM vs. BM

Q. What are honorifics?

One thing that makes the Korean language difficult is honorifics. Mainly, honorifics are how one speaks to people whom are older. The opposite of honorifics is casual speech. This is how older people will speak to younger people in many circumstances. In South Korea, age is a very important factor in socializing. This is why not using honorifics can be considered rude and offensive.

So let's take a look at how you can introduce yourself to people your age.

A

난 캐런이야.

(Nahn kae-ruh-nee-yah.)

B

전 캐런이에요.

(Juhn kae-ruh-nee-eh-yoh.)

Both A and B say 'I am Karen.' Notice how the first word changed from 난 (nahn) to 전 (juhn). This is the honorific version of the word 난 (nahn), which means 'I.' Also, the end of B is slightly different and longer than the end of A. This form of speech is called 존댓말 (john-daet-mahl) a.k.a. honorifics. The opposite of 존댓말 (john-daet-mahl) is 반말 (bahn-mahl).

The actual meanings of A and B are exactly the same. But if you are speaking to an older person, B is the right way of speaking. (You can use A for talking to a younger person or person of the same age.) However, honorifics should be used when you meet someone for the first time whether the person is older or younger. To make things even more complicated, it is generally considered customary for grown-ups to speak in casual speech when meeting and talking to a child for the first time. This is why sometimes even Koreans have trouble deciding which style of speech should be used.

Q. What are JDM and BM?

From this point forward, let's call honorifics or 존댓말 (john-daet-mahl) 'JDM.' There was an American singer and songwriter named John Denver, whom passed away many years ago. If he were still alive today, he would be over 70 years old. So most people would be using JDM ("John Denver Mahl") toward John Denver.

On the other hand, 'BM' or 반말 (bahn-mahl) is the way you talk to your friends, siblings, and cousins. We can call it "Bieber Mahl" after Justin Bieber. (Again, you should not be using BM the first time you meet someone. JDM should be used instead.)

Q. How do I know if someone is using JDM?

The easiest way to tell is to see if the person is ending each sentence with "요 (yoh)." Remember how you can say hello in Korean? In BM, it is 안녕 (ahn-nyuhng). In JDM, it is 안녕하세요 (ahn-nyuhn-hah-seh-yoh). Almost always, the JDM version is longer than the BM version.

As an example, 잘 있었어요? (Jah ree-ssuh-ssuh-yoh?) is the JDM form whereas 잘 있었어? (Jah ree-ssuh-ssuh?) is considered BM. Both sentences mean 'Have you been well?'

Q. Should I use JDM or BM when it is not clear whether I am younger or older than the person I am speaking to?

Now this is interesting. Every now and then, you might run into a tricky situation. The general rule is use JDM if you are not sure. It is better to be overly polite than be impolite. This is why many Koreans ask for the other person's age when they meet someone for the first time. To ask for someone's age, you can say the following.

A

나이가 어떻게 되세요?

(Nah-ee-gah uh-dduh-keh dweh-seh-yoh?)

B

연세가 어떻게 되세요?

(Yuhn-seh-gah uh-dduh-keh dweh-seh-yoh?)

Use A when asking someone whom looks around your age. If the person looks to be around your father's or mother's age, then B is considered more polite. 연세 (yuhn-seh) is the honorific version of 나이 (nah-ee), which means 'age' in Korean. Both A and B are in JDM.

7. How to Start Sentences

Q. How do sentences start in Korean?

The word order of Korean sentences is very different from English sentences.

He went home.

In this English sentence, the first word is the subject of the sentence. In other words, this sentence is about 'he.' The second word is the main verb, followed by an object noun. This word order is known as SVO, meaning Subject-Verb-Object. In Korean, however, the word order is slightly different. It is SOV or Subject-Object-Verb. Now let's translate this sentence into Korean.

그는 집에 갔어.

(Geu-neun jee-beh gah-ssuh.)

그는 (geu-neun) means 'he,' which is the subject of the sentence. 집에 (jee-beh) is an object noun, meaning 'home.' 갔어 (gah-ssuh) is the main verb. It means 'went.' So the word order has changed from SVO to SOV.

He home went.

This is the default word order of Korean. Sentences in Korean usually begin with nouns and almost always end with verbs. This is why most Korean textbooks will use SOV sentences as examples. However, spoken Korean is somewhat different. People will usually omit the subject word when they speak. This is because the SOV style is too formal for conversation. So SOV becomes just OV with no subject. That means we have to take out 그는 (geu-neun) from the sentence above to make it sound more casual and conversational.

집에 갔어.

(Jee-beh gah-ssuh.)

Korean is usually spoken this way, which is the reason why pronouns such as 'I,' 'you,' 'he,' and 'she' are rarely used.

Q. But how can a sentence make sense if it does not have a subject?

It is not all that difficult to guess what the subject is. Let's look at an example.

영화 봤어.

(Yuhng-hwah bwah-ssuh.)

영화 (yuhng-hwah) means 'movie' and 봤어 (bwah-ssuh) means 'saw.' So the sentence says 'Saw a movie.' But who saw the movie? Clearly, the sentence does not state the person of interest. The subject could be 'I,' 'you,' or something else. But the listener will likely know the answer. Here is a possible conversation taking place between Mary and Erica.

Mary: 어저께 뭐 했어? (Uh-juh-ggeh mwuh hae-ssuh?)

Erica: 영화 봤어. (Yuhng-hwah bwah-ssuh.)

Here are the translations.

Mary: What did (subject) do yesterday?

Erica: (Subject) watched a movie.

Even though the subject can be anyone, it is very likely that Erica is talking about herself. If Mary wanted to ask about someone else, she would have used a specific word for the subject. Let's say Mary was asking about Erica's brother, Kyle. Now the sentence would start with the subject.

Mary: 카일은 어저께 뭐 했어? (Kah-ee-reu nuh-juh-ggeh mwuh hae-ssuh?)

Erica: 영화 봤어. (Yuhng-hwah bwah-ssuh.)

Notice how Erica's response is still missing a subject. Once again, it is because the subject is implied. Since Mary asked about Kyle, Erica's answer would be about him as well. It will be quite strange for Erica to talk about another person when Mary specifically asked about Kyle. But what if Erica does not know what Kyle did the day before?

Mary: 카일은 어저께 뭐 했어? (Kah-ee-reu nuh-juh-ggeh mwuh hae-ssuh?)

Erica: 몰라. (Mohl-lah.)

몰라 (mohl-lah) means 'don't know.' In this context, Erica is talking about herself and not Kyle. Erica is the one who doesn't know what Kyle did yesterday. But she did not declare the subject since it is pretty obvious she meant she doesn't know and not Kyle.

Q. What are some other examples of OV sentences?

Let's look at the following sentences with no subjects.

1. 뭐 해? (Mwuh hae?)

뭐 (mwuh) = what

해 (hae) = do

2. 거의 다 왔어. (Guh-eui dah wah-ssuh.)

거의 (guh-eui) = almost

다 (dah) = completely

왔어 (wah-ssuh) = arrived

3. 별로야. (Byuhl-loh-yah.)

별로 (byuhl-loh) = so so

-야 (-yah) = is

4. 언제 왔니? (Uhn-jeh waht-nee?)

언제 (uhn-jeh) = when

왔니 (what-nee) = arrived?

5. 방금 시작했어. (Bahng-geum shee-jah-kae-ssuh.)

방금 (bahng-geum) = just now

시작했어 (shee-jah-kae-ssuh) = started

8. How to End Sentences

Q. How do sentences end in Korean?

In Korean, sentences usually end with verbs. This is true even if the sentence is a question. Let's take a look at the following JDM sentence.

비가 와요.

(Bee-gah wah-yoh.)

비가 (bee-gah) is 'rain' and 와요 (wah-yoh) is the JDM version of 'come' or 'is coming.' When you hear a verb, you will know that is the end of the sentence.

Q. Is there an easy way of telling which words are verbs?

Korean sentences will almost always end with verbs. Of course, there are a few exceptions.

진짜? (Jeen-jjah?) = Really?

네. (Neh.) = Yes.

왜? (Wae?) = Why?

As you can see, these sentences are one-word expressions. In typical sentences with more words, verbs come at the very end. JDM sentences usually end with a "다 (dah)" or "요 (yoh)" sound. Verbs in BM sentences have too many ending-sounds to list here.

9. Subjects & Objects

Q. How can I tell subject nouns apart from object nouns?

Now you know Korean sentences can be SOV or OV. However, some sentences are SV (Subject-Verb) and have no object.

비가 온다.

(Bee-gah ohn-dah.)

비 (bee), meaning 'rain' in Korean, is the subject. 온다 (ohn-dah) is the main verb, meaning '(is) coming.' Put them together and we have 비가 온다 (bee-gah ohn-dah), which means 'it's raining.' Technically, 비 (bee) could be an object noun. So how do we know which one it is? The answer has to do with suffixes. Also known as particles, suffixes are attached at the end of nouns. They determine whether a noun is a subject or object word. Here are the main suffixes.

Subject suffixes: -이/-가 (-ee/-gah), -은/-는 (-eun/-neun)

Object suffixes: -을/-를 (-eul/-reul)

If a noun ends with -이 (-ee), -가 (-gah), -은 (-eun), or -는 (-neun), then it becomes the subject of a sentence. If it ends with -을 (-eul) or -를 (-reul), that would mean it is an object. Let's try adding a suffix to the word 'tree.'

Tree as the subject: 트리가 (teu-ree-gah), 트리는 (teu-ree-neun)

Tree as an object: 트리를 (teu-ree-reul)

If you were to start a sentence with 'tree' as the subject, you can either say 트리가 (teu-ree-gah) or 트리는 (teu-ree-neun). If 'tree' becomes an object noun, then 트리를 (teu-ree-reul) should be used. (In casual speech, suffixes are often omitted for convenience.)

Q. What is the difference between -이 (-ee) and -가 (-gah)?

Basically, -이 (-ee) is used for words that end with closed (consonant) sounds whereas -가 (-gah) is used for words ending with open (vowel) sounds. They function the same way, but using the wrong suffix will make a sentence almost incomprehensible. This is true for -은/-는 (-eun/-neun) and -을/-를 (-eul/-reul) as well.

For the following, can you guess which group needs -이 (-ee) and which group needs -가 (-gah)?

Group A

거울 (guh-wool)

신발 (sheen-bahl)

음악 (eu-mahg)

책 (chaeg)

돌 (dohl)

Group B

종이 (johng-ee)

포도 (poh-doh)

키 (kee)

나무 (nah-moo)

유리 (you-ree)

Try attaching **-가** (-gah) at the end of each word in Group A. Then try the same with **-이** (-ee). Which one sounds natural? Here are the same words with the right suffixes.

Group A

거울이 (guh-woo-ree)

신발이 (sheen-bah-ree)

음악이 (cu mɑh ghee)

책이 (chae-ghee)

돌이 (doh-ree)

Group B

종이가 (johng-ee-gah)

포도가 (poh-doh-gah)

키가 (kee-gah)

나무가 (nah-moo-gah)

유리가 (you-ree-gah)

We can do the same with -은 (-eun) and -는 (-neun).

Group A

거울은 (guh-woo-reun)

신발은 (sheen-bah-reun)

음악은 (eu-mah-geun)

책은 (chae-geun)

돌은 (doh-reun)

Group B

종이는 (johng-ee-neun)

포도는 (poh-doh-neun)

키는 (kee-neun)

나무는 (nah-moo-neun)

유리는 (you-ree-neun)

Korean speakers do not think about which suffix to use for each word. Once you get used to it, you won't have to think about it either. Practice is the key.

Q. How are -이/-가 (-ee/-gah) different from -은/-는 (-eun/-neun)?

This question gets asked fairly often and it is one of the most difficult concepts to explain. Technically, -이/-가 (-ee/-gah) and -은/-는 (-eun/-neun) have the same purpose; they make a noun the subject of a sentence. So why are there two different sets? Let's look at the following.

A

낸시가 놀랐다.

(Naen-ssee-gah nohl-laht-ddah.)

B

낸시는 놀랐다.

(Naen-ssee-neun nohl-laht-ddah.)

낸시 (naen-ssee) or 'Nancy' can be followed by either -가 (-gah) or -는 (neun). This is because 'Nancy' ends with an open sound. 놀랐다 (nohl-laht-ddah) means 'was surprised.' So both A and B can be used to mean 'Nancy was surprised.' The subtle difference may be that A describes Nancy's state from a third-person's perspective. On the other hand, B sees Nancy from oneself's point of view. Imagine watching Nancy with a friend. You can describe Nancy's state to your friend by saying A. But if you are looking at Nancy by yourself, you might have a thought in your head as B.

In general, you can use -이/-가 (-ee/-gah) for describing actions and -은/-는 (-eun/-neun) for describing states or conditions. Being surprised is an internal state and not an action. So B should be used here. However, you can still use A since -이/-가 (-ee/-gah) and -은/-는 (-eun/-neun) are usually interchangeable.

Here is another example.

A

조던이 노래했다.

(Joh-duh-nee noh-rae-haet-ddah.)

B

조던은 노래했다.

(Joh-duh-neun noh-rae-haet-ddah.)

조던 (joh-dun) or 'Jordan' has a closed sound at the end, so -이 (-ee) and -은 (-eun) are the correct suffixes. Both A and B mean 'Jordan sang (a song).' Singing is an action and not a state. So A sounds better in this case.

But what about using B in this context? It is also grammatically correct. However, B seems as if there is an underlying meaning to it. (e.g Jordan sang as he was being executed.)

There is no clear rule when it comes to differentiating -이/-가 (-ee/-gah) and -은/-는 (-eun/-neun). Listening to people's conversations is the only way of getting used to using right suffixes.

Q. What is the difference between -을 (-eul) and -를 (-reul)?

-을 (-eul) and -를 (-reul) actually have the same function. But words can only be followed by one of them. Let's take the same nouns as before and turn them into object words.

Group A

거울은 (guh-woo-reun)

신발은 (sheen-bah-reun)

음악은 (eu-mah-geun)

책은 (chae-geun)

돌은 (doh-reun)

Group B

종이는 (johng-ee-neun)

포도는 (poh-doh-neun)

키는 (kee-neun)

나무는 (nah-moo-neun)

유리는 (you-ree-neun)

So -이 (-ee) and -은 (-eun) are used for consonant-ending nouns and -가 (-gah) and -는 (-neun) are used for vowel-ending nouns. (By the way, the words in Group A mean 'mirror,' 'shoe,' 'music,' 'book,' 'rock' and the words in Group B mean 'paper,' 'grape,' 'height,' 'tree,' and 'glass,' respectively.)

There are a countless number of other suffixes in Korean. This is one area where many people feel overwhelmed when they are learning Korean for the first time. Fortunately, you don't have to learn them all at the same time. We will discuss more about Korean particles in Chapter 32.

10. How to Introduce Yourself

Q. How can I introduce myself in Korean?

I think we are now ready to start and finish a sentence in Korean. So let's try one. If you want to introduce yourself to people your age, all you have to say is 난 (nahn), your name, and then -야 (-yah) or -이야 (-ee-yah) like the following.

A

난 (nahn) + your name + -야 (-yah)

B

난 (nahn) + your name + -이야 (-ee-yah)

The word order is SOV. If your name ends with an open sound, use A. If it ends with a closed sound, use B. Let's say your name is Sarah. The name ends with "ah," which is an open sound. This means we should go with A.

Sarah: 난 사라야. (Nahn sah-rah-yah.)

Let's try the same with a few other names.

Chris: 난 크리스야. (Nahn keu-ree-sseu-yah.)

Mary: 난 메리야. (Nahn meh-ree-yah.)

Mike: 난 마이크야. (Nahn mah-ee-keu-yah.)

Emily: 난 에밀리야. (Nah neh-meel-lee-yah.)

How about names like John, Bob, Karen, and Tom? Since these names end with closed sounds, we should use B.

John: 난 존이야. (Nahn joh-nee-yah.)

Bob: 난 밥이야. (Nahn bab-bee-yah.)

Karen: 난 캐런이야. (Nahn kae-ruh-nee-yah.)

Tom: 난 톰이야. (Nahn toh-mee-yah.)

Here we used -이야 (-ee-yah) instead of -야 (-yah). All of these sentences are in BM. (There is no -요 (-yoh) at the end of each sentence.) That means you should not be using these sentences toward people you just met.

Q. How do I introduce myself to people whom are older?

If you want to introduce yourself to a stranger or someone who is much older than yourself, then you must speak in JDM. Here are the names of the Muindo characters from the EASY KOREAN channel on YouTube.

Jaesik: 재식 (jae-sheeg)

Mansu: 만수 (mahn-soo)

Bahb-oh: 밥오 (bah-boh)

Hyungdol: 형돌 (hyuhng-dohl)

Ddongchil: 똥칠 (ddohl-cheel)

Hehe: 헤헤 (heh-heh)

Let's use these names to make JDM sentences. Again, we have two options.

A

전 (juhn) + your name + -예요 (-yeah-yoh)

B

전 (juhn) + your name + -이에요 (-ee-eh-yoh)

The 'I' pronoun changed from 난 (nahn) to 전 (juhn), which is the honorific version of 난 (nahn). The endings also changed to include -요 (-yoh). For vowel-ending names, use A. If your name ends with a consonant, use B. Here are a few examples.

Jaesik: 전 재식이에요. (Juhn jae-shee-ghee-eh-yoh.)

Mansu: 전 만수예요. (Juhn mahn-soo-yeah-yoh.)

Bahb-oh: 전 **밥오예요**. (Juhn bah-boh-yeah-yoh.)

Hyungdol: 전 **형돌이에요**. (Juhn hyuhng-doh-ree-eh-yoh.)

Ddongchil: 전 **똥칠이에요**. (Juhn ddohng-chee-ree-eh-yoh.)

Hehe: 전 **헤헤예요**. (Juhn heh-heh-yeah-yoh.)

11. Top Three Verbs

Q. What are some of the most common Korean verbs?

Let's first go through three basic Korean verbs.

-다/-이다 (-dah/-ee-dah)

아니다 (ah-nee-dah)

하다 (hah-dah)

-다 (-dah) is the 'be verb' in Korean. It is used as 'am,' 'are,' and 'is.' If the word that precedes -다 (-dah) ends with an open sound, then -이 (-ee) is added to become -이다 (-ee-dah). So for words like 'cat,' 'milk,' 'fan,' and 'tool,' use -이다 (-ee-dah) instead.

Cat: 캣이다 (kae-shee-dah)

Milk: 밀크이다 (meel-keu-ee-dah)

Fan: 팬이다 (pae-nee-dah)

Tool: 툴이다 (too-ree-dah)

For words like 'tree,' 'umbrella,' 'sky,' and 'Chicago,' use -다 (-dah) and not -이다 (-ee-dah).

Tree: 트리다 (teu-ree-dah)

Umbrella: 엄브렐라다 (uhm-beu-rehl-lah-dah)

Sky: 스카이다 (seu-kah-ee-dah)

Chicago: 시카고다 (shee-kah-goh-dah)

Let's say you are walking in a park and you spot a rabbit. You can point to the rabbit and say the following.

토끼다!

(Toh-gghee-dah!)

The sentence says 'It's a rabbit!" It combined 토끼 (toh-gghee), which is 'rabbit' in Korean, and -다 (-dah) as the 'be' verb. (There is no translation for 'a' since Korean does not make use of articles such as 'a,' 'an,' and 'the.')

Q. What is 아니다 (ah-nee-dah)?

아니다 (ah-nee-dah) is the opposite of -다/-이다 (-dah/-ee-dah). When you say 아니다 (ah-nee-dah), you are saying something is 'not.' Let's go back to the park. Maybe what you saw was actually a cat. Then what can you say?

토끼가 아니다.

(Toh-gghee-gah ah-nee-dah.)

아니다 (ah-nee-dah) is used as a separate word, which functions as the main verb. 토끼 (toh-gghee) is followed by **-가** (-gah), indicating this noun is the subject. You can also say the following.

토끼가 아니야.

(Toh-gghee-gah ah-nee-yah.)

The ending changed from **-다** (-dah) to **-야** (yah). The former is the default version whereas the latter is a casual version in BM. **아니다** (ah-nee-dah), **아니야** (ah-nee-yah), and **아니예요** (ah-nee-yeah-yoh) all have the same meaning.

Q. What is 하다 (hah-dah)?

하다 (hah-dah) is the Korean word for 'do.' **-다/-이다** (-dah/-ee-dah) and **아니다** (ah-nee-dah) describe something's or someone's states or conditions. On the other hand, **하다** (hah-dah) describes actions or physical movements.

노래하다.

(Noh-rae-hah-dah.)

노래 (noh-rae) means 'song.' So **노래하다** (noh-rae-hah-dah) means 'do song' or 'sing.' In English, a word like 'cook' can be either a noun or verb. In Korean, a noun becomes a verb when it is followed by **하다** (hah-dah). This is why many Korean verbs are simply nouns plus **하다** (hah-dah). Let's see a few more examples of a noun turning into a verb.

숙제 (soog-jjeh): 숙제하다 (soog-jjeh-hah-dah) = do (one's) homework

설거지 (suhl-guh-jee): 설거지하다 (suhl-guh-jee-hah-dah) = do the dishes

게임 (ggeh-eem): 게임 하다 (ggeh-eem hah-dah) = play a game

A noun and 하다 (hah-dah) can be considered one word with no space between them or two words with a space. Basically, all three examples show how nouns can become verbs in Korean. If you know the noun, you also know the verb. Pretty neat, isn't it?

12. Sentence Structure

Q. How can I say the day of the week in Korean?

We can either use SOV or OV to tell the day of the week. For instance, let's look at the following.

SOV: **오늘은 월요일이야**. (Oh-neu-reu nwuh-ryoh-ee-ree-yah.)

OV: **월요일이야**. (Wuh-ryoh-ee-ree-yah.)

오늘 (oh-neul) means 'today' and **월요일** (wuh-ryoh-eel) means 'Monday.' Both sentences are written in BM. In the SOV sentence, the -**은** (-eun) suffix is attached to **오늘** (oh-neul). That would make this word the subject. Since the subject is already established now, **월요일** (wuh-ryoh-eel) has to be an object.

-**이야** (-ee-yah) is a form of -**이다** (-ee-dah) in BM. The OV sentence is the same as the SOV sentence except that it is missing the subject. So which of the two sentences is correct?

The SOV sentence looks like it is something from a Korean classroom. Even though it is not wrong, it still sounds way too formal for people to use it. In spoken Korean, the OV sentence would be the right choice.

Let's say Henry asked his friend, Kyle, a question.

Henry: **오늘 무슨 요일이야**? (Oh-neul moo-seu nyoh-ee-ree-yah?)

무슨 (moo-seun) means 'what.' So Henry is asking for the day of the week. Kyle can respond by saying one of the two.

Kyle: 월요일이야. (Wuh-ryoh-ee-ree-yah.)

Kyle: 월요일. (Wuh-ryoh-eel.)

The second option is more commonly used between friends. But what if Henry and Kyle are strangers? Then his response should be in JDM. (The question asked by Henry should also be in JDM.)

Henry: 오늘 무슨 요일이에요? (Oh-neul moo-seu nyoh-ee-ree-eh-yoh?)

Kyle: 월요일이요. (Wuh-ryoh-ee-ree-yoh.)

If Kyle simply says 월요일 (Wuh-ryoh-eel) as a response, it will be considered BM and not JDM. Thus -이요 (-ee-yoh) must be attached at the end to not be offensive.

Here are the entire days of the week in JDM.

월요일이에요. (Wuh-ryoh-ee-ree-eh-yoh.) = It's Monday.

화요일이에요. (Hwah-yoh-ee-ree-eh-yoh.) = It's Tuesday.

수요일이에요. (Soo-yoh-ee-ree-eh-yoh.) = It's Wednesday.

목요일이에요. (Moh-gyoh-ee-ree-eh-yoh.) = It's Thursday.

금요일이에요. (Geu-myoh-ee-ree-eh-yoh.) = It's Friday.

토요일이에요. (Toh-yoh-ee-ree-eh-yoh.) = It's Saturday.

일요일이에요. (Ee-ryoh-ee-ree-eh-yoh.) = It's Sunday.

Q. How can I say 'I'm not an American' in Korean?

We've already covered the verb 아니다 (ah-nee-dah), which means 'not.' So let's try making a sentence that means 'I'm not an American' by using this word. But, first, let's take a look at the following sentence.

저는 미국인이에요.

(Juh-neun mee-goo-ghee-nee-eh-yoh.)

저는 (juh-neun) is 'I' in JDM and 미국인 (mee-goo-gheen) means 'American.' -이에요 (-ee-eh-yoh) is a JDM form of -이다 (-ee-dah), meaning 'am.'

I + American + am

=

I am (an) American

Where can we insert 아니다 (ah-nee-dah) in this sentence to make it mean the opposite? Since the verb is placed at the end, it should come after 미국인 (mee-goo-gheen). This means we should take out the original verb, -이에요 (-ee-eh-yoh).

저는 미국인이 아니에요.

(Juh-neun mee-goo-ghee-nee ah-nee-eh-yoh.)

Let's see what the sentence looks like in BM.

난 미국인이 아니야.

(Nahn mee-goo-ghee-nee ah-nee-yah.)

난 (nahn) is the short version of 나는 (nah-neun). For 저는 (juh-neun), it is 전 (juhn). They all have the same meaning.

Q. How can I make commands in Korean?

In English, you make a command sentence by putting the main verb in the beginning. In Korean, the word order stays the same whether it is SOV, SV, or OV. The difference is the way the verb conjugates or changes at the end. Let's see how we can say 'call me' in Korean.

전화하다.

(Juhn-hwah-hah-dah.)

This sentence is a combination of 전화 (juhn-hwah) and 하다 (hah-dah). 전화 (juhn-hwah) means 'phone' or 'call' as a noun. 하다 (hah-dah) means 'do.' By putting them together, they turn into a verb. But this sentence is not a command just yet. To make it into a command, we must change 하다 (hah-dah).

전화해.

(Juhn-hwah-hae.)

해 (hae) is 하다 (hah-dah) as a command in BM. What would it look like in JDM?

전화하세요.

(Juhn-hwah-hah-seh-yoh.)

하세요 (hah-seh-yoh) is 하다 (hah-dah) as a command in JDM. However, here is a better way of say-ing it.

전화주세요.

(Juhn-hwah-joo-seh-yoh.)

주세요 (joo-seh-yoh) is a command form of 주다 (joo-dah) in JDM. It means 'give.' So 전화주세요 (Juhn-hwah-joo-seh-yoh) means '(please) give a call.' 주세요 (joo-seh-yoh) is more of a request whereas 하세요 (hah-seh-yoh) is more of an order. So in JDM, people tend to use 전화주세요 (juhn-hwah-joo-seh-yoh) instead of using 전화하세요 (juhn-hwah-hah-seh-yoh).

13. I in Korean

Q. How can I say 'I,' 'my,' 'me,' and 'mine' in Korean?

There are two ways of saying the first-person pronouns, BM and JDM. First, let's take a look at the words in BM.

I: 나는 (nah-neun), 내가 (nae-gah)

My: 내 (nae)

Me: 나한테 (nah-hahn-teh)

Mine: 내 거 (nae gguh)

Unlike the rest, 'I' comes in two forms. Use 나는 (nah-neun) to describe something about yourself. For actions, use 내가 (nae-gah). By the way, both 나는 (nah-neun) and 내가 (nae-gah) are with suffixes. Without the suffixes, they are just 나 (nah) and 내 (nae).

Here are example sentences of the first-person pronouns in Korean.

나는 오빠가 있어. (Nah-neu noh-bbah-gah ee-ssuh.) = I have an older brother.

내가 전화할게. (Nae-gah juhn-hwah-hahl-ggeh.) = I will call you.

내 폰 어디갔지? (Nae poh nuh-dee-gaht-jjee?) = Where did my phone go?

나한테 물어봐. (Nah-hahn-teh moo-ruh-bwah.) = Ask me.

그건 내 거 아니야. (Geu-guhn nae gguh ah-nee-yah.) = That is not mine.

Here are the same words in JDM.

I: 저는 (juh-neun), 제가 (jeh-gah)

My: 제 (jeh)

Me: 저한테 (juh-hahn-teh)

Mine: 제 거 (jeh gguh)

Everything is the same except the words now start with ㅈ (jeu) and not ㄴ (neu).

저는 지금 집이에요. (Juh-neun jee-geum jee-bee-eh-yoh.) = I am home right now.

제가 도와 드릴게요. (Jeh-gah doh-wah deu-reel-ggeh-yoh.) = I will help you.

제 이름 아세요? (Jeh ee-reu mah-seh-yoh?) = Do you know my name?

엄마가 저한테 말했어요. (Uhm-mah-gah juh-hahn-teh mahl-hae-ssuh-yoh.) = Mom said to me.

제 거 아닌 거 같습니다. (Jeh gguh ah-neen guh gaht-sseub-nee-dah.) = I don't think it is mine.

Notice how almost every one of them ends with -요 (-yoh), which is a quick way of telling if a sentence is in JDM.

Q. What is the difference between 나는 (nah-neun) and 난 (nahn)?

Just like how 'I am' can be shortened into 'I'm,' 나는 (nah-neun) can also be used as 난 (nahn). Of course, the meaning stays exactly the same. 난 (nahn) is more commonly used in spoken Korean than 나는 (nah-neun). This shortening method works for many other Korean pronouns.

14. You in Korean

Q. What does 니가 (nee-gah) mean in Korean?

Before we discuss what 'niga' means in Korean (hint: it's not what you think), let's first talk about the second-person pronouns.

You: 너는 (nuh-neun), 네가 (neh-gah)

Your: 네 (neh)

You: 너한테 (nuh-hahn-teh)

Yours: 네 거 (neh gguh)

These words are very similar to the ones from the last chapter, so make sure you don't confuse them. For instance, it might be difficult to tell 내가 (nae-gah) and 네가 (neh-gah) apart. So most Koreans developed a habit of pronouncing the word 네가 (neh-gah) as "니가 (nee-gah)." Technically speaking, 니가 (nee-gah) is not the correct spelling or pronunciation of the word 'you' in Korean. (But most Korean songs will use this word instead so that there is no confusion.)

The JDM forms of the second-person pronouns are almost never used. Usually, it is considered impolite to call someone 'you' in JDM. If you are curious, 너 (nuh) in JDM is 당신 (dahng-sheen).

So, to answer the original question, "니가 (nee-gah)" refers to the person you are speaking to and nothing else.

Q. Then how can I make sentences in JDM without using the word 'you?'

Instead of saying 'you' in JDM, Korean speakers would use the OV style to speak. Let's take a look at an example.

You can do it.

How would you translate this sentence into Korean? There are two answers.

A

너는 할 수 있어.

(Nuh-neun hahl ssoo ee-ssuh.)

B

당신은 하실 수 있어요.

(Dahng-shee-neun hah-sheel ssoo ee-ssuh-yoh.)

Clearly, A is in BM and B is in JDM. In B, **너** (nuh) is replaced by **당신** (dahng-sheen) and the sentence ends with **-요** (-yoh). But no one would actually say it. To make the sentence sound natural, we should take out the subject. Once again, Korean is often spoken without the subject.

하실 수 있어요.

(Hah-sheel ssoo ee-ssuh-yoh.)

This sounds a lot more natural. (If you must use a word to describe the person, then you would have to call the person by different words in different situations.)

Q. Can 너는 (nuh-neun) be shortened as well?

Yes. Just like 난 (nahn) exists for 나는 (nah-neun), 넌 (nuhn) can be used in place of 너는 (nuh-neun).

너는 누구야?

(Nuh-neun noo-goo-yah?)

넌 누구야?

(Nuhn noo-goo-yah?)

Both sentences mean 'Who are you?'

15. He & She in Korean

Q. How can I say 'he' and 'she' in Korean?

In English, a sentence usually starts with the subject.

John went to Singapore.

Then you can replace the name with the pronoun 'he' for the rest of the conversation.

He will be back in three days.

However, there is no need for words like 'he' and 'she' in Korean. Usually, the subject is implied once it is established. First, let's take a look at the following.

A

존은 싱가포르에 갔어.

(Joh-neun ssing-gah-poh-reu-eh gah-ssuh.)

존 싱가포르 갔어.

(John ssing-gah-poh-reu gah-ssuh.)

In many Korean books, you will see sentences written like A. However, it sounds very formal. That is why B is more commonly used. Well, what is the difference between the two? B has no suffixes. Notice how -은 (-eun) and -에 (-eh) are missing in B. (Even though this can be considered improper, most people speak this way.)

Once the listener understands that the speaker is talking about John, the subject can be dropped completely.

삼 일 뒤에 올 거야.

(Sah meel dwee-eh ohl gguh-yah.)

This sentence starts with **삼 일** (sah meel), which means 'three days.' The subject, John, is not mentioned. This is why the third-person pronouns like 'he' and 'she' are almost never used. Still, let's go through them. (You don't have to memorize all of these words.)

He: **그는** (geu-neun), **그가** (geu-gah)

His: **그의** (geu-eui)

Him: **그한테** (geu-hahn-teh)

His: **그의 거** (geu-eui gguh)

She: 그녀는 (geu-nyuh-neun), 그녀가 (geu-nyuh-gah)

Her: 그녀의 (geu-nyuh-eui)

Her: 그녀한테 (geu-nyuh-hahn-teh)

Hers: 그녀의 거 (geu-nyuh-eui gguh)

As long as you remember 그 (geu) means 'boy' or 'man' and 그녀 (geu-nyuh) means 'girl' or 'woman,' you can just skip the rest of the words. Let's try another example to see how this works.

수지 어디 갔어?

(Soo-jee uh-dee gah-ssuh?)

수지 (soo-jee) is a girl's name. 어디 (uh-dee) means 'where' and 갔어 (gah-ssuh) means 'went.' So the sentence says 'Where did Suzy go?' Let's assume 수지 (soo-jee) went to the park. 'Park' in Korean is 공원 (gohng-wuhn). Here are possible answers.

A: 수지는 공원에 갔어. (Soo-jee-neun gohng-wuh-neh gah-ssuh.)

B: 그녀는 공원에 갔어. (Geu-nyuh-neun gohng-wuh-neh gah-ssuh.)

C: 수지 공원 갔어. (Soo-jee gohng-wuhn gah-ssuh.)

D: 그녀 공원 갔어. (Geu-nyuh gohng-wuhn gah-ssuh.)

E: 공원에 갔어. (Gohng-wuh-neh gah-ssuh.)

F: 공원 갔어. (Gohng-wuhn gah-ssuh.)

They all say the same thing; that Suzy went to the park. But A and B are way too formal. Not only they have suffixes, but they also show the subject. These choices might be considered correct on Korean language exams. But no Korean speakers would actually speak this way.

C and D, on the other hand, are missing suffixes. However, they still have the subject (SOV). So they do not sound right either, just like A and B.

E and F are how one would speak in real life. (F sounds more natural, but E also works.)

16. We in Korean

Q. How can I say 'we,' 'our,' 'us,' and 'ours' in Korean?

The 'we' pronouns in Korean can also be said in two different ways. Here are the BM versions. Make sure you know these words since they are used a lot.

We: 우리는 (woo-ree-neun), 우리가 (woo-ree-gah)

Our: 우리의 (woo-ree-eui)

Us: 우리한테 (woo-ree-hahn-teh)

Ours: 우리 거 (woo-ree gguh)

우리는 (woo-ree-neun) can be shortened to 우린 (woo-reen). One of the reasons why 우리 (woo-ree) is common is because it can also mean 'my' in addition to meaning 'our.' For example, most Korean speakers would say 우리 엄마 (woo-ree uhm-mah) instead of saying 내 엄마 (nae uhm-mah) when referring to one's own mother. But wouldn't 우리 엄마 (woo-ree uhm-mah) mean 'our mom' and not 'my mom?' Depending on the situation, it can mean one or the other.

If two sisters are talking about their mother, then 우리 엄마 (woo-ree uhm-mah) would mean 'our mom.' But if two friends are talking, then one of them can say 우리 엄마 (woo-ree uhm-mah) to mean her own mother ('my mom' and not 'our mom'). Consider 우리 (woo-ree) as an affectionate term for a close person. (Keep in mind that this word is BM and should not be used in JDM speech.) Here are common ways of describing personal relationships. You can think of it as 내 (nae) vs. 우리 (woo-ree).

My dad: 우리 아빠 (woo-ree ah-bbah)

My mom: 우리 엄마 (woo-ree uhm-mah)

My older brother: 우리 오빠 (woo-ree oh-bbah) / 우리 형 (woo-ree hyuhng)

My older sister: 우리 언니 (woo-ree uhn-nee) / 우리 누나 (woo-ree noo-nah)

My younger brother/sister: 우리 동생 (woo-ree dohng-saeng) or 내 동생 (nae dohng-saeng)

My husband: 우리 남편 (woo-ree nahm-pyuhn) or 내 남편 (nae nahm-pyuhn)

My wife: 우리 아내 (woo-ree ah-nae) or 내 아내 (nae ah-nae)

If you are female, you say 우리 오빠 (woo-ree oh-bbah) and 우리 언니 (woo-ree uhn-nee). If you are male, then use 우리 형 (woo-ree hyuhng) and 우리 누나 (woo-ree noo-nah) to mean 'my older brother' and 'my older sister,' respectively.

Now let's see how 우리 (woo-ree) looks like in JDM.

We: 저희는 (juh-heui-neun), 저희가 (juh-heui-gah)

Our: 저희의 (juh-heui-eui)

Us: 저희한테 (juh-heui-hahn-teh)

Ours: 저희 거 (juh-heui gguh)

Let's say you and your friend want to tell an elderly Korean woman that you are from Thailand or 태국 (tae-goog).

A

우리는 태국에서 왔어요.

(Woo-ree-neun tae-goo-geh-suh wah-ssuh-yoh.)

B

저희는 태국에서 왔어요.

(Juh-heui-neun tae-goo-geh-suh wah-ssuh-yoh.)

Which one is better? The verb at the end, **왔어요** (wah-ssuh-yoh), indicates both sentences are indeed in JDM. However, because **우리** (woo-ree) is considered very casual, B is more proper than A is.

17. They in Korean

Q. How often words like 'they' and 'them' are used in Korean?

In English, the word 'they' is used for talking about specific groups of people like children, athletes, customers, students, etc. However, it is not the case for Korean. Either the subject is not spoken or another word is used. Before we take a look at example sentences, let's first go through the third-person plural pronouns in BM.

They: 그들은 (geu-deu-reun), 그들이 (geu-deu-ree)

Their: 그들의 (geu-deu-reui)

Them: 그들한테 (geu-deul-hahn-teh)

Theirs: 그들 거 (geu-deul gguh)

Here are the JDM forms.

They: 그분들은 (geu-boon-deu-reun), 그분들이 (geu-boon-deu-ree)

Their: 그분들의 (geu-boon-deu-reui)

Them: 그분들한테 (geu-boon-deul-hahn-teh)

Theirs: 그분들 거 (geu-boon-deul gguh)

The JDM versions are the same as the BM versions except that 분 (boon) is added. Now let's see how English sentences are translated into Korean sentences.

A: They left. = 떠났어. (Dduh-nah-ssuh.)

B: This is their classroom. = 여기가 교실입니다. (Yuh-ghee-gah gyoh-shee-reeb-nee-dah.)

C: I can't see them. = 안 보여. (Ahn boh-yuh.)

D: Mine is bigger than theirs. = 내 거가 더 커요. (Nae gguh-gah duh kuh-yoh.)

All of the four translations in Korean are missing pronouns. In C, not only 'them' is gone, but 'I' is missing as well. In a Korean textbook, the sentence would have been written as the following.

나는 그들이 안 보여.

(Nah-neun geu-deu-ree ahn boh-yuh.)

But this is way too formal for it to be spoken. If you really want to have a subject in place, then you can use 그 사람들 (geu sah-rahm-deul) instead of 그들 (geu-deul). 그 사람들 (geu sah-rahm-deul) means 'the people' and it is used more often.

If the word 'they' is used to mean things and not people, then you may use the following.

They: 그것들은 (geu-guht-ddeu-reun), 그것들이 (geu-guht-ddeu-ree)

Them: 그것들 (geu-guht-ddeul)

These words are the same in both BM and JDM. However, they are rarely used in Korean. The Korean language usually does not separate singular nouns from plural nouns. In other words, objects (things) usually stay singular even though there are more than one.

For instance, one 'apple' in Korean is 사과 (sah-gwah). Two 'apples' is still 사과 (sah-gwah). If you really want to pluralize the word, then you can say 사과들 (sah-gwah-deul). However, plural forms for objects are not common in Korean.

18. Other Pronouns

Q. How can I say 'this,' 'that,' and 'it' in Korean?

These pronouns are very common in everyday Korean. Since they refer to things like cars and phones, there is no distinction between BM and JDM. Let's take a look.

This: **이거** (ee-guh) / **이것** (ee-guht)

That: **저거** (juh-guh) / **저것** (juh-guht)

It: **그거** (geu-guh) / **그것** (geu-guht)

There is not much difference between **이거** (ee-guh) and **이것** (ee-guht). In written Korean, **이것** (ee-guht) is preferred. In speech, **이거** (ee-guh) is way more prevalent. The same applies for **저거** (juh-guh) and **그거** (geu-guh).

This: **이거 맛있어**. (Ee-guh mah-shee-ssuh.)

That: **저거 맛있어**. (Juh-guh mah-shee-ssuh.)

It: **그거 맛있어**. (Geu-guh mah-shee-ssuh.)

맛있어 (mah-shee-ssuh) means 'delicious.' Now you probably know what they mean. Let's try another set. This time, we will use **것** (guht).

This: 이것 좀 먹어 봐. (Ee-guht jjohm muh-guh bwah.)

That: 저것 좀 먹어 봐. (Juh-guht jjohm muh-guh bwah.)

It: 그것 좀 먹어 봐. (Geu-guht jjohm muh-guh bwah.)

좀 (johm) is a word used for commands or asking for favors. (It works similarly to the word 'please' in English.) 먹어 봐 (muh-guh bwah) means 'try eating.' Here are the same sentences in JDM.

This: 이것 좀 드세요. (Ee-guht jjohm deu-seh-yoh.)

That: 저것 좀 드세요. (Juh-guht jjohm deu-seh-yoh.)

It: 그것 좀 드세요. (Geu-guht jjohm deu-seh-yoh.)

The verb has changed in all three sentences, but the rest is the same. Again, these pronouns can be used in both BM and JDM.

Q. What about 'these' and 'those' in Korean?

If you want to say 'this cup' in Korean, you can say 이 컵 (ee cuhb). But how would you say 'these cups' in Korean? There are two choices, singular and plural.

Singular: 이 컵 (ee cuhb)

Plural: 이 컵들 (ee cuhb-ddeul)

The suffix -들 (-deul) implies that there is more than one cup. It is the same way with 'that' and 'those' in Korean.

Singular: 저 컵 (juh cuhb)

Plural: 저 컵들 (juh cuhb-ddeul)

Since it is usually not necessary to use the plural form in Korean, you can use either one.

Let's try one more example. How can you say 'this person' and 'these people' in Korean? By the way, 'person' in Korean is 사람 (sah-rahm).

This person: 이 사람 (ee sah-rahm)

These people: 이 사람들 (ee sah-rahm-deul)

That person: 저 사람 (juh sah-rahm)

Those people: 저 사람들 (juh sah-rahm-deul)

The person: 그 사람 (geu sah-rahm)

The people: 그 사람들 (geu sah-rahm-deul)

The JDM word for 'person' is 분 (boon). For instance, 이 사람들 (ee sah-rahm-deul) in JDM is 이 분들 (ee boon-deul). 분 (boon) is used a lot for discussing the number of customers at a restaurant.

19. More Verbs

Q. What are some other verbs in Korean?

We've already covered three verbs; -이다 (-ee-dah), 아니다 (ah-nee-dah), and 하다 (hah-dah). Now let's add five more to the list. (For a complete list of basic Korean verbs, purchase Korean Words with Cat Memes 2/5.)

있다 (eet-ddah): This word either means 'there is (object)' or someone 'has (object).' 티켓이 있다 (tee-keh-shee eet-ddah) would mean somebody has a ticket. But what about 곰이 있다 (goh-mee eet-ddah)? 곰 (gohm) means 'bear' in Korean. Even though it can mean someone owns a bear, it is more likely to mean 'there is a bear.' 있다 (eet-ddah) is the default form. In BM, it is 있어 (ee-ssuh). In JDM, the word changes to 있어요 (ee-ssuh-yoh). For now, let's focus on the default forms.

가다 (gah-dah): It means 'go.' For example, 학교에 가다 (hahg-ggyoh-eh gah-dah) means '(subject) goes to school.'

마시다 (mah-shee-dah): This verb means 'drink.' Do not confuse 마시다 (mah-shee-dah) with 맛있다 (mah-sheet-ddah), which means something 'is delicious.'

먹다 (muhg-ddah): It means 'eat' or 'drink.' Unlike in English, you can use this verb to mean both. Many Korean speakers would say 물 먹어 (mool muh-guh) to tell someone to drink water. 마시다 (mah-shee-dah), on the other hand, specifically means 'drink' and nothing else.

같다 (gaht-ddah): This word means something is either 'similar' or 'same.' If one says 이름이 같다 (ee-reu-mee gaht-ddah), it likely means two people have the same name.

Q. Why do so many Korean sentences end with -네요 (-neh-yoh)?

A Korean verb is almost never spoken in its default form. Let's look at 노래하다 (noh-rae-hah-dah) as an example.

형진이가 노래하다.

(Hyung-jee-nee-gah noh-rae-hah-dah.)

This sentence means either 'Hyungjin sings' or 'Hyungjin is singing.' But since the verb is not conjugated, we have to change it.

형진이가 노래한다.

(Hyung-jee-nee-gah noh-rae-hahn-dah.)

Can you find the difference? -하다 (-hah-dah) has changed to -한다 (-hahn-dah). This is a perfectly usable form. However, what if we were to switch this sentence into JDM?

A

형진이가 노래해요.

(Hyung-jee-nee-gah noh-rae-hae-yoh.)

B

형진이가 노래하네요.

(Hyung-jee-nee-gah noh-rae-hah-neh-yoh.)

Both A and B are common. However, A sounds a bit more basic than B does. That is why many Korean speakers would use B instead. Changing the ending of a verb to -네요 (-neh-yoh) does not necessarily change the meaning. It just happens to be a common way of conjugating verbs. -네요 (-neh-yoh) in BM is just -네 (-neh), which is also very common.

20. Asking Questions

Q. How can I ask questions in Korean?

Mainly, there are two types of questions based on how they can be answered. Some questions have to be answered with full sentences. But there are also questions that can simply be answered with 'yes' or 'no.' So let's find out how you can say 'yes' and 'no' in Korean? First, here are the words in BM.

Yes: 어 (uh), 응 (eung)

No: 아니 (ah-nee)

Both 어 (uh) and 응 (eung) can be used interchangably. The JDM versions are the following.

Yes: 네 (neh), 예 (yeah)

No: 아니요 (ah-nee-yoh)

Again, 네 (neh) and 예 (yeah) mean 'yes' in JDM. They are both very common.

Now let's see how we can turn a sentence into a question.

집에 갔다.

(Jee-beh gaht-ddah.)

집 (jeeb) means 'house' or 'home.' 갔다 (gaht-ddah) is the past tense of 가다 (gah-dah). So the sentence indicates that somebody 'went home.' To make it sound more conversational, let's change 갔다 (gaht-ddah) to 갔어 (gah-ssuh).

집에 갔어.

(Jee-beh gah-ssuh.)

Now how do we turn it into a question? Well, nothing really has to change. The word order stays the same as before. But for it to be a question, you would raise the tone at the end of the sentence.

집에 갔어?

(Jee-beh gah-ssuh?)

Can't be any simpler, can it? But does it work with the original sentence with 갔다 (gaht-ddah) in its default form?

집에 갔다?

(Jee-beh gaht-ddah?)

Unfortunately, this will not work. In general, the verb has to be conjugated before it turns into a typical question. Let's take a look at the JDM form of the original sentence and turn it into a question.

집에 갔습니다.

(Jee-beh gaht-sseub-nee-dah.)

Since this sentence also ends with -다 (-dah), we would have to change the ending as well. There are two ways of doing it.

A

집에 갔어요.

(Jee-beh gah-ssuh-yoh.)

B

집에 기셨어요.

(Jee-beh gah-shuh-ssuh-yoh.)

If the person who went home is around your age, use A. If the person is somewhat older, then use B. (Technically, the person has to be even older than the listener you are speaking to if you want to use B.) How would you turn A and B into questions? Now it is very simple. Just say them out loud like they are questions.

A

집에 갔어요?

(Jee-beh gah-ssuh-yoh?)

B

집에 가셨어요?

(Jee-beh gah-shuh-ssuh-yoh?)

To answer, you can use 네 (neh), 예 (yeah), or 아니요 (ah-nee-yoh). For the BM question, you can use 어 (uh), 응 (eung), or 아니 (ah-nee).

Q. What about questions that start with 'what,' 'where,' 'who,' etc.?

WH questions start with specific words such as 'who' and 'when.' Let's see what they are in Korean.

What: 뭐 (mwuh) / 무엇 (moo-uht)

Who: 누가 (noo-gah)

Where: 어디 (uh-dee)

When: 언제 (uhn-jeh)

Why: 왜 (wae)

Which: 어느 (uh-neu)

How: 어떻게 (uh-dduh-keh)

Let's try asking questions in JDM using these words. (The verbs will stay BM, which are common for couples and peers in the beginning of their relationships.)

뭐 해요? (Mwuh hae-yoh?) = What are you doing?

어디 가요? (Uh-dee gah-yoh?) = Where are you going?

언제 와요? (Uhn-jeh wah-yoh?) = When is he coming?

누구세요? (Noo-goo-seh-yoh?) = Who are you?

왜 웃어요? (Wae woo-suh-yoh?) = Why are you laughing?

어느 게 내 거예요? (Uh-neu geh nae gguh-yeah-yoh?) = Which is mine?

어떻게 먹어요? (Uh-dduh-keh muh-guh-yoh?) = How do I eat this?

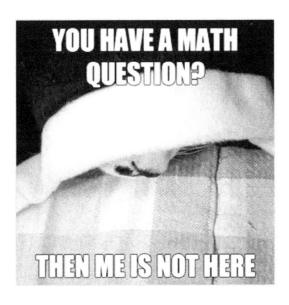

21. Korean Prepositions

Q. What are some of the Korean prepositions?

In English, words like 'in,' 'on,' 'to,' 'from,' and 'for' are placed prior to nouns. Since they are positioned before nouns, they are known as prepositions. In Korean, prepositions come after nouns. So they are called postpositions even though their roles are the same. Here are five common prepositions, or postpositions, in Korean.

In: 안에 (ah-neh)

On: 위에 (wee-eh)

To: -에/-게 (-eh/-geh), -로/-으로 (-roh/-eu-roh)

From: -에서 (-eh-suh), -한테 (-hahn-teh)

For: 위한 (wee-hahn), 동안 (dohng-ahn)

Q. How are postpositions used in sentences in Korean?

Let's take a look at the following English sentence.

The ball is in the box.

What would this sentence look like in Korean? Let's keep the words 'ball' and 'box' in English to make things easier. In Hangul, 'ball' is 볼 (bohl) and 'box' is 박스 (bahg-sseu). The 'is' in this sentence will turn into 있다 (eet-ddah). The preposition 'In' is 안에 (ah-neh). (We don't have to translate 'the.')

볼 있다 안에 박스.

(Boh reet-ddah ah-neh bahg-sseu.)

But this sentence is not in the right order. So let's change the word order from SVO to SOV.

볼 안에 박스 있다.

(Boh rah-neh bahg-sseu eet-ddah.)

This looks much better. However, there is a major flaw in translation. This sentence says the box is in the ball, which is the opposite of what we want to say. To mean 'in the box' in Korean, we have to put the preposition come after the noun.

볼 박스 안에 있다.

(Bohl bahg-sseu ah-neh eet-ddah.)

We are almost complete, but there is still a problem. The subject is followed by an object, which is confusing because they are both nouns. So we should attach -이/-가 (-ee/-gah) for the subject.

볼이 박스 안에 있다.

(Boh-ree bahg-sseu ah-neh eet-ddah.)

If we use Korean words for 'ball' and 'box,' then we get the following.

공이 상자 안에 있다.

(Gohng-ee sahng-jah ah-neh eet-ddah.)

Here are more examples of other postpositions.

위에 (wee-eh): 책상 위에 있어. (Chaeg-ssahng wee-eh ee-ssuh.)

-에/-게 (-eh/-geh): 학교에 갔어요. (Hah-ggyoh-eh gah-ssuh-yoh.)

-로/-으로 (-roh/-eu-roh): 큰 길로 갔어요. (Keun gheel-loh gah-ssuh-yoh.)

-에서 (-eh-suh): 유럽에서 왔어. (You-ruh-beh-suh wah-ssuh.)

-한테 (-hahn-teh): 엄마한테 전화왔어. (Uhm-mah-hahn-teh juhn-hwah-wah-ssuh.)

위한 (wee-hahn): 헨리를 위한 거야. (Hehn-ree-reul wee-hahn guh-yah.)

동안 (dohng-ahn): 삼 일 동안 아팠어요. (Sah meel ddohng-ahn ah-pah-ssuh-yoh.)

Don't worry about what these sentences mean for now. Instead, try to see how each postposition is placed after a noun.

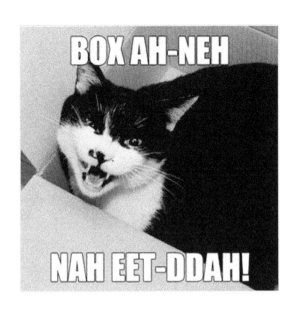

22. Korean Conjunctions

Q. How do I use conjunctions in Korean?

Conjunctions are words that connect words, phrases, and sentences together. The most common conjunctions in English are 'and,' 'or,' 'but,' and 'so.' Korean conjunctions work pretty much the same way. Let's take a look.

And: 그리고 (geu-ree-goh), -과/-와 (-gwah/-wah)

But: 그런데 (geu-ruhn-deh), 하지만 (hah-jee-mahn)

Or: 아니면 (ah-nee-myuhn), -나/-이나 (-nah/-ee-nah)

So: 그래서 (geu-rae-suh)

그리고 (geu-ree-goh), 'and' in Korean, is usually not used in its full form. It often merges with a verb to be a single word. (This is possible because the main verb comes at the end of the sentence in Korean.) So it usually just becomes -고 (-goh), which is attached to the verb at the end of the sentence. Here are a few examples.

Eat: 먹다 (muhg-ddah)

Eat and: 먹고 (muhg-ggoh)

Go: 가다 (gah-dah)

Go and: 가고 (gah-goh)

Study: 공부하다 (gohng-boo-hah-dah)

Study and: 공부하고 (gohng-boo-hah-goh)

This is a convenient way to connect two verbs together. Let's take a look at the following for an example.

밥 먹고 가.

(Bahb muhg-ggoh gah.)

밥 (bahb) is 'rice' or 'meal.' 먹고 (muhg-ggoh) is 먹다 (muhg-ddah) plus -고 (-goh); in other words, 'eat and.' 가 (gah) is a command form of 가다 (gah-dah) in BM. So what does the sentence say? It mean you should have a meal and then go. (It is a way of asking a guest to stay longer at one's home.)

-과 (-gwah) and -와 (-wah) also mean 'and,' but they usually come between two nouns. -와 (-wah) is used when it is followed by a noun that ends with an open sound. -과 (-gwah) is used when the previous word ends with a closed sound.

Tom and Jerry: 톰과 제리 (tohm-gwah jeh-ree)

Jerry and Tom: 제리와 톰 (jeh-ree-wah tohm)

그런데 (geu-ruhn-deh) and 하지만 (hah-jee-mahn) both mean 'but' in Korean. However, 그런데 (geu-ruhn-deh) can also be used when a person wants to say something slightly different. In other words, 그런데 (geu-ruhn-deh) can mean 'I know, but...' whereas 하지만 (hah-jee-mahn) would sound more strongly opinionated. Another Korean word of 'but' is 그러나 (geu-ruh-nah). However, this word is mostly used in written materials such as books.

The word 'or' in Korean also has two different forms. 아니면 (ah-nee-myuhn) is used to mean just 'or' whereas -나 (-nah) and -이나 (-ee-nah) are used to mean 'either A or B.' Let's try a quiz to see how they are used.

Do you want vanilla (1) chocolate ice-cream?

I don't mind vanilla (2) chocolate.

Is 아니면 (ah-nee-myun) a better fit for (1) or (2)? How about -나 (-nah) and -이나 (-ee-nah)? In (1), you have to choose one or the other. So 아니면 (ah-nee-myun) should go in. However, in (2), the person is saying either vanilla or chocolate is fine. Since the noun 'vanilla' ends with an open sound, -나 (-nah) would be the right suffix.

그래서 (geu-rae-suh) is used almost the same way the word 'so' is used in English. It can also mean 'then' as well.

그래서 어떻게 됐어?

(Geu-rae-suh uh-dduh-keh dwae-ssuh?)

어떻게 (uh-dduh-keh) means 'how' and 됐어 (dwae-ssuh) is a form of 되다 (dweh-dah) in BM, which means 'become' or 'happen.' This sentence can either mean 'So what happened?' or 'Then what happened?'

23. Past Tense Verbs

Q. How can I change tenses of Korean verbs?

In English, 'run' becomes 'ran' as it becomes past tense. The meaning of the word stays the same. The only difference is whether the course of action takes place in the future, present, or past. Korean verbs work exactly the same way. A verb in the past tense will usually have an 었 (uht), 였 (yuht), or 았 (aht) sound. Let's see how 'is' can turn into 'was' in Korean.

Present tense: -다/-이다 (-dah/-ee-dah)

Past tense: -었다/-이었다 (-uht-ddah/-ee-uht-ddah)

Here is a sentence in the present tense.

가을이다.

(Gah-eu-ree-dah.)

가을 (gah-eul) means 'fall' or 'autumn.' So this sentence means 'It's fall.' How would you change the verb ending to the past tense? Simply replace -이다 (-ee-dah) with -이었다 (-ee-uht-ddah).

가을이었다.

(Gah-eu-ree-uht-ddah.)

Now the sentence says 'It was fall,' making it about the past. Let's take a look at another verb.

Present tense: **아니다** (ah-nee-dah)

Past tense: **아니었다** (ah-nee-uht-ddah)

Here, we see the same pattern. **-다** (-dah) is replaced by **-었다** (-uht-ddah).

정답이 아니다.

(Juhng-dah-bee ah-nee-dah.)

This sentence means 'It is not the right answer.' Now how we change it to 'It was not the right answer?'

정답이 아니었다.

(Juhng-dah-bee ah-nee-uht-ddah.)

But this is not really how people speak because of **-다** (-dah). This is only the official form of verbs. So let's try changing the endings of these two sentences.

정답이 아니야.

(Juhng-dah-bee ah-nee-yah.)

정답이 아니었어.

(Juhng-dah-bee ah-nee-uh-ssuh.)

These sentences are in BM. In JDM, this is what they look like.

정답이 아니에요.

(Juhng-dah-bee ah-nee-eh-yoh.)

정답이 아니었어요.

(Juhng-dah-bee ah-nee-uh-ssuh-yoh.)

How would the verb 하다 (hah-dah), meaning 'do,' become the past tense?

Present tense: 하다 (hah-dah)

Past tense: 하였다 (hah-yuht-ddah), 했다 (haet-ddah)

했다 (haet-ddah) is simply a shorter version of 하였다 (hah-yuht-ddah). Here is a JDM sentence in the present tense.

쇼핑해요.

(Ssyoh-ping-hae-yoh.)

쇼핑 (ssyoh-ping) is how 'shopping' is pronounced in Korean. So the sentence means 'I shop' or 'I'm shopping' at the moment. (Technically, it can also be used to mean 'let's shop.') Now let's try turning the sentence into the past tense. We have two choices in JDM.

쇼핑하였어요.

(Ssyoh-ping-hah-yuh-ssuh-yoh.)

쇼핑했어요.

(Ssyoh-ping-hae-ssuh-yoh.)

Both sentences mean 'I did shopping' or 'I went shopping.' However, the second one is much more common when it is spoken. Here are the same sentences in BM.

쇼핑하였어.

(Ssyoh-ping-hah-yuh-ssuh.)

쇼핑했어.

(Ssyoh-ping-hae-ssuh.)

Again, the shorter sentence is more commonly spoken.

Q. What are the past tenses of other verbs?

We have covered a few other Korean verbs in Chapter 19. Let's take a look at what their past tenses look like.

Present tense: 있다 (eet-ddah)

Past tense: 있었다 (ee-ssuht-ddah)

Present tense: 가다 (gah-dah)

Past tense: 갔다 (gaht-ddah)

Present tense: 마시다 (mah-shee-dah)

Past tense: 마셨다 (mah-shuht-ddah)

Present tense: 먹다 (muhg-ddah)

Past tense: 먹었다 (muh-guht-ddah)

Present tense: 같다 (gaht-ddah)

Past tense: 같았다 (gah-taht-ddah)

Verbs are usually spoken in the past tense or future tense, so it is very important to know how they change.

24. Future Tense Verbs

Q. How can I say 'I will' or 'I am going to' in Korean?

Let's list the future tense verbs in BM the way they are actually used in conversations.

Present tense: -이다 (-ee-dah)

Future tense: -일 거야 (-eel gguh-yah)

Present tense: 아니다 (ah-nee-dah)

Future tense: 아닐 거야 (ah-neel gguh-yah)

Present tense: 하다 (hah-dah)

Future tense: 할 거야 (hahl gguh-yah)

Present tense: 마시다 (mah-shee-dah)

Future tense: 마실 거야 (mah-sheel gguh-yah)

Present tense: 걷다 (guht-ddah)

Future tense: 걸을 거야 (guh-reul gguh-yah)

Present tense: 오다 (oh-dah)

Future tense: 올 거야 (ohl gguh-yah)

Present tense: 가다 (gah-dah)

Future tense: 갈 거야 (gahl gguh-yah)

Present tense: 공부하다 (gohng-boo-hah-dah)

Future tense: 공부할 거야 (gohng-boo-hahl gguh-yah)

Present tense: 일하다 (eel-hah-dah)

Future tense: 일할 거야 (eel-hahl gguh-yah)

Pretty easy, right? If you hear a "gguh" sound right at the end of a sentence, there is a good chance the verb is in the future tense.

25. Helping Verbs

Q. Does the Korean language have helping verbs?

Words like 'can,' 'should,' 'will,' and 'must' are known as helping verbs or auxiliary verbs. They are usually placed before the main verb. Let's take a look at the following example.

I can ride a bicycle.

In this sentence, the word 'can' assists the main verb 'ride.' In Korean, helping verbs and regular verbs are usually attached together. Also, the helping verb comes after the main verb and not before. Let's try to translate the sentence above into Korean.

난 자전거를 탈 줄 알아.

(Nahn jah-juhn-guh-reul tahl jjoo rah-rah.)

자전거 (jah-juhn-guh) is 'bicycle.' The main verb here is 타다 (tah-dah), meaning 'ride.' The auxiliary verb is 알다 (ahl-dah). This verb usually means 'know,' but it can also mean 'know how to' or 'can' as a helping verb. 타다 (tah-dah) plus 알다 (ahl-dah) becomes 탈 줄 알다 (tahl jjoo rahl-dah). Some Korean textbooks may use 탈 수 있다 (tahl ssoo eet-ddah), which also works.

Q. What are some common Korean helping verbs?

The most common one is 보다 (boh-dah). When the verb is used by itself, it means 'see.' But when it is used as a helping verb, it means 'try.' Let's combine a regular verb, 먹다 (muhg-ddah), with this helping verb.

먹어 보다.

(Muh-guh boh-dah.)

To make 먹다 (muhg-ddah) the main verb, the form changed to 먹어 (muh-guh). The sentence means 'try eating.' But sentences usually do not end with -다 (-dah) when they are spoken. To make it sound more conversational, 보다 (boh-dah) should be changed to 봐 (bwah). In JDM, it should be 보세요 (boh-seh-yoh.)

먹어 봐.

(Muh-guh bwah.)

먹어 보세요.

(Muh-guh boh-seh-yoh.)

The verb, 먹어 (muh-guh), should be changed to 드셔 (deu-shuh) to make the sentence completely JDM.

드셔 보세요.

(Deu-shuh boh-seh-yoh.)

Let's see how 보다 (boh-dah) is used with three other verbs.

마시다 (mah-shee-dah) + 보다 (boh-dah): 마셔 보다 (mah-shuh boh-dah)

가다 (gah-dah) + 보다 (boh-dah): 가 보다 (gah boh-dah)

걷다 (guht-ddah) + 보다 (boh-dah): 걸어 보다 (guh-ruh boh-dah)

마시다 (mah-shee-dah) means 'drink,' 가다 (gah-dah) means 'go,' and 걷다 (guht-ddah) means 'walk.'

Another common helping verb is 주다 (joo-dah). As a regular verb, it means 'give.' As a helping verb, however, 주다 (joo-dah) means 'help' or 'assist.' Here are a few examples in BM and JDM.

도와 줘. (Doh-wah jwuh.) = Help me.

읽어 주세요. (Eel-guh joo-seh-yoh.) = Read it to me.

먹어 줘. (Muh-guh jwuh.) = Eat it for me.

와 주세요. (Wah joo-seh-yoh.) = Come to me.

26. Negative Sentences

Q. What are 못 (moht) and 안 (ahn) and how are they different?

To make sentences mean the opposite in Korean, we can use either 못 (moht) or 안 (ahn). Both of these adverbs are used to make verbs negative. Let's look at a sentence in Korean.

못 먹다.

(Moht muhg-ddah.)

먹다 (muhg-ddah) means 'eat.' By placing 못 (moht) before the main verb, it changes the meaning of the clause to 'cannot eat.' How would you tell someone in Korean that you can't eat shrimp? By the way, 'shrimp' in Korean is 새우 (sae-woo).

전 새우 못 먹어요.

(Juhn sae-woo moht muh-guh-yoh.)

The word order here is SOV; 'I,' 'shrimp,' 'cannot,' and 'eat.' How would the meaning of this sentence change if we replace 못 (moht) with 안 (ahn)?

전 새우 안 먹어요.

(Juhn sae-woo ahn muh-guh-yoh.)

This sentences no longer means 'I can't eat shrimp.' Instead, it means 'I don't eat shrimp' or 'I won't eat shrimp.' So 안 (ahn) is used to mean 'do not' or 'will not.' You can think of 안 (ahn) as 아니다 (ah-nee-dah) being a helping verb. Whereas 안 (ahn) means 'do not' or 'will not,' 아니다 (ah-nee-dah) means 'is not.' Let's look at the following example.

A

오늘은 화요일이야.

(Oh-neu-reun hwah-yoh-ee-ree-yah.)

B

오늘은 화요일이 아니야.

(Oh-neu-reun hwah-yoh-ee-ree ah-nee-yah.)

A says 'Today is Tuesday' and B says 'Today is not Tuesday.'

가지 않다.

(Gah-jee ahn-tah.)

This sentence uses 않- (ahn-), which is different from 안 (ahn) and 아니다 (ah-nee-dah); as if things weren't confusing enough. Just remember that there are two words that sound like "ahn" in Korean. Even though 안 (ahn) and 않- (ahn-) are different, beginners can treat them as the same word since they are used in a similar style. One major difference is 안 (ahn) is a separate word whereas 않- (ahn-) attaches itself to the beginning of a word as a prefix. By the way, 가지 않다 (gah-jee ahn-tah) means someone 'does not go.'

117

27. Small Numbers

Q. How can I count numbers in Korean?

There are a couple of different ways of counting numbers in Korean. So it can be somewhat confusing in the beginning. To make matters worse, unique counting words exist for different objects. But we could make things easier by taking it one concept at a time. First, let's start with the Korean number words from zero to ten.

0: 공 (gohng), 영 (young)

1: 일 (eel), 한/하나 (hahn/hah-nah)

2: 이 (ee), 두/둘 (doo/dool)

3: 삼 (sahm), 세/셋 (seh/seht)

4: 사 (sah), 네/넷 (neh/neht)

5: 오 (oh), 다섯 (dah-suht)

6: 육 (youg), 여섯 (yuh-suht)

7: 칠 (cheel), 일곱 (eel-gohb)

8: 팔 (pahl), 여덟 (yuh-duhl)

9: 구 (goo), 아홉 (ah-hohb)

10: 십 (sheeb), 열 (yuhl)

So you might be wondering why they are two different sets of number words. The first set is based on Chinese characters and the second set is strictly Korean. The general rule is use the Chinese-based number words for big numbers and use the Korean-based number words for small numbers. (You can memorize them more easily by counting with your fingers.) So how would 'three apples' be translated into Korean?

사과 세 개

(sah-gwah seh gae)

사과 (sah-gwah) is 'apple' and 세 (seh) is 'three.' So what is 개 (gae) at the end? Basically, 개 (gae) is a general count word for objects. Unlike English, counting words (also known as classifiers) exist for Korean and other Asian languages as well. They are always followed by numbers. So instead of putting 'three' before 'apples,' you start with 'apples' first and then say 'three,' which is followed by a count word such as 개 (gae). If a number is not followed by a counting word, then 세 (seh) becomes 셋 (seht). (This only applies to some numbers and not all.)

사과 삼 개

(sah-gwah sahm gae)

This phrase also says 'three apples,' but it uses a Chinese-based number, 삼 (sahm). Even though people will still understand what it means, the sentence does sound somewhat strange. If the number is smaller than 20 or 30, the Korean-based number words are used more often than not. If the number is bigger than 50, Chinese-based number words are almost always the right choice.

Q. What are some common counting words in Korean?

Different counting words exist for counting the number of people, trees, books, clothes, cars, etc. English speakers may not be familiar with this concept. But the most important part is the number itself. So you can safely assume whatever follows the number is a count word. Here is a list of the most common counting words in Korean. (By far, 개 (gae) is the most popular one. It also means 'dog.')

People: 명 (myuhng)

Animals: 마리 (mah-ree)

Trees: 그루 (geu-roo)

Flowers: 송이 (sohng-ee)

Books: 권 (gwuhn)

Pages: 장 (jahng)

Cars: 대 (dae)

Clothes: 벌 (buhl)

Years old (age): 살 (sahl), 세 (seh)

두 명이요.

(Doo myuhng-ee-yoh.)

This is something you can say when you go to a restaurant to tell the waitperson how many people you are with, including yourself. Do not make the mistake of using 개 (gae) or 마리 (mah-ree) for 명

(myung). When counting the number of people, the only words you can use are 명 (myung) and 분 (boon). Consider 분 (boon) as the JDM version of 명 (myung). For example, the waitperson may use 분 (boon) and not 명 (myung) toward customers to be extra polite.

18살이에요.

(Yuhl-lyuh-duhl-ssah-ree-eh-yoh.)

'Years old' in Korean is either 살 (sahl) or 세 (seh). 세 (seh) is much more formal than 살 (sahl) and is not as common. If you want to ask someone for his or her age, you can say the following.

A

몇 살이야?

(Myuht ssah-ree-yah?)

B

나이가 어떻게 되세요?

(Nah-ee-gah uh-dduh-kae dweh-seh-yoh?)

나이 (nah-ee) means 'age.' 어떻게 (uh-dduh-kae) means 'how' or 'what.' So A sounds more like 'How old are you?' when B is more of saying 'What is your age?' Clearly, A is BM where as B is JDM. (A is mostly used by adults speaking toward children or teenagers.)

Q. How do I say numbers bigger than ten in Korean?

Just like before, we have two different sets of words for 'ten,' 'eleven,' 'twenty,' 'thirty,' and so on.

11: **십일** (shee-beel), **열한/열하나** (yuhl-hahn/yuhl-hah-nah)

12: **십이** (shee-bee), **열두/열둘** (yuhl-ddoo/yuhl-ddool)

13: **십삼** (sheeb-ssahm), **열세/열셋** (yuhl-sseh/yuhl-sseht)

14: **십사** (sheeb-ssah), **열네/열넷** (yuhl-neh/yuhl-neht)

15: **십오** (shee-boh), **열다섯** (yuhl-ddah-suht)

16: **십육** (sheem-nyoug), **열여섯** (yuhl-lyuh-suht)

17: **십칠** (sheeb-cheel), **열일곱** (yuh-reel-gohb)

18: **십팔** (sheeb-pahl), **열여덟** (yuhl-lyuh-duhl)

19: **십구** (sheeb-ggoo), **열아홉** (yuh-rah-hohb)

20: **이십** (ee-sheeb), **스무/스물** (seu-moo/seu-mool)

'Eleven' in Korean is basically a combination of 'ten' and 'one' for both sets; **십** (sheeb) plus **일** (eel) and **열** (yuhl) plus **하나** (hah-nah). This rule works for the rest of the numbers above except for **스물** (seu-mool).

Q. How can I say words like 'first,' 'second,' and 'third' in Korean?

Here is how to say 'first' to 'tenth' in Korean. For these words, only one set exists.

First: 첫 번째 (chuht bbuhn-jjae)

Second: 두 번째 (doo buhn-jjae)

Third: 세 번째 (seh buhn-jjae)

Fourth: 네 번째 (neh buhn-jjae)

Fifth: 다섯 번째 (dah-suht bbuhn-jjae)

Sixth: 여섯 번째 (yuh-suht bbuhn-jjae)

Seventh: 일곱 번째 (eel-gohb bbuhn-jjae)

Eighth: 여덟 번째 (yuh-duhl bbuhn-jjae)

Ninth: 아홉 번째 (ah-hohb bbuhn-jjae)

Tenth: 열 번째 (yuhl bbuhn-jjae)

번째 (buhn-jjae) indicates 'order' or the number of 'times' of something. 처음 (chuh-eum) can be used to mean 첫 번째 (chuht bbuhn-jjae).

28. Big Numbers

Q. How can I tell big numbers in Korean?

In the previous chapter, we talked about Korean number words between zero and twenty. Now let's talk about bigger numbers. (We do not have to memorize the Korean-based number words anymore since they are not nearly as popular as the Korean-based ones.)

30: 삼십 (sahm-sheeb)

40: 사십 (sah-sheeb)

50: 오십 (oh-sheeb)

60: 육십 (youg-sseeb)

70: 칠십 (cheel-sseeb)

80: 팔십 (pahl-sseeb)

90: 구십 (goo-sheeb)

100: 백 (baeg)

1,000: 천 (chuhn)

10,000: 만 (mahn)

100,000: 십만 (sheeb-mahn)

1,000,000: 백만 (baeg-mahn)

10,000,000: 천만 (chuhn-mahn)

100,000,000: 억 (uhg)

1,000,000,000: 십억 (shee-buhg)

Let's take a look at more naturally occuring numbers.

32: 삼십이 (sahm-shee-bee)

48: 사십팔 (sah-sheeb-pahl)

85: 팔십오 (pahl-ssee-boh)

120: 백이십 (bae-ghee-sheeb)

2,000: 이천 (ee-chuhn)

56,000: 오만육천 (oh-mah-nyoug-chuhn)

300,000: 삼십만 (sahm-sheeb-mahn)

5,500,000: 오백오십만 (oh-bae-goh-sheeb-mahn)

Q. Do I really need to know such huge numbers?

The answer is yes. It is mostly because of the Korean currency, the won or 원 (wuhn). Approximately, one U.S. dollar is worth about 1,000 won. How much does a cup of coffee cost? Perhaps five dollars. That would be 5,000 won. How about a brand new car with a 30,000-dollar price tag? In the Korean currency, it might cost over 30 million won.

It can be overwhelming at first to work with such big numbers, but there are a couple of benefits from doing so. Your math skills might improve because you get to use large numbers regularly. Also, you can become a millionaire in South Korea with only a thousand dollars!

29. Korean Adjectives

Q. How are adjectives used in Korean?

Adjectives like 'pretty,' 'fun,' and 'thirsty' generally describe nouns. They are used as a way of expressing one's thoughts or feelings. Without adjectives, it will be extremely difficult to talk about anything in detail. Korean adjectives have the same job, but they appear completely different from English adjectives. Here is one example.

목이 길다.

(Moh-ghee gheel-dah.)

목 (mohg) means 'neck,' which is followed by a suffix -이 (-ee). This makes the noun the subject of the sentence. 길다 (gheel-dah) means something 'is long.' Traditional Korean grammar classifies this word as an adjective, but it clearly looks like a verb. If we say 길다 (gheel-dah) is an adjective, then the sentence above does not contain any verb. So, from now on, Korean adjectives are going to be considered adjective verbs.

There is a different way of using adjectives in Korean. It is a lot more similar to how adjectives are used in English.

긴 목

(gheen mohg)

긴 (gheen) is a form of 길다 (gheel-dah) strictly as an adjective and not as an adjective verb. It is placed before the noun, 목 (mohg). It literally translates to 'long neck' in English. However, this wording style is not nearly as common as the style of 길다 (gheel-dah). So let's just focus on adjective verbs for now.

A

맛있다.

(Mah-sheet-ddah.)

B

맛없다.

(Mah-duhb-ddah.)

Here, we have just one word for each sentence. Both words are adjective verbs. A means 'delicious' whereas B means something is 'not delicious.' The subject is absent and implied, but it is safe to assume the sentences are describing some food item.

Q. What are some common Korean adjectives?

Let's look at the following three common adjectives verbs.

예쁘다

(yeah-bbeu-dah)

This word means 'pretty.' So how would you say 'She is pretty' in Korean?

그녀는 예쁘다.

(Geu-nyuh-neu nyeah-bbeu-dah.)

그녀는 이쁘다.

(Geu-nyuh-neu nee-bbeu-dah.)

그녀 (geu-nyuh) is 'she' and -는 (-neun) shows 그녀 (geu-nyuh) is the subject and not an object. Even though 예쁘다 (yeah-bbeu-dah) is the correct spelling and pronunciation, many people have developed of a habit of using 이쁘다 (ee-beau-dah) instead. So the second sentence is more commonly spoken compared to the first one, even though the meaning does not change.

좋다

(joh-tah)

This means 'good.' It is usually used as 좋아 (joh-ah) in BM and 좋아요 (joh-ah-yoh) in JDM.

나쁘다

(nah-bbeu-dah)

This word is the opposite of 좋다 (joh-tah), meaning 'bad.' In BM, the form changes to 나빠 (nah-bbah). In JDM, it is 나빠요 (nah-bbah-yoh). This word is not as common as you might think, because it is way too straight forward and sounds a little too extreme. So many people would say 안 좋다 (ahn joh-tah) instead, which means 'not good.'

YOUR HAND ISN'T SO

MAH-SHEET-DDAH

30. Korean Adverbs

Q. What are some of common Korean adverbs?

Five to ten adverbs are used a lot in Korean. (In English, words like 'well,' 'more,' 'fast,' and 'very' are considered common adverbs.) Unlike adjectives, adverbs describe many types of words (e.g. verbs). Adverbs are very common in the Korean language, so let's take a look at a few.

Well: 잘 (jahl)

Really: 진짜 (jeen-jjah)

A lot, many, much: 많이 (mah-nee)

Fast, quickly: 빨리 (bbahl-lee)

Very: 굉장히 (gwehng-jahng-hee)

잘 (jahl) is one of the most common Korean adverbs. It is as popular as the adjective 'good' in English. In contrast, 좋다 (joh-tah), an adjective verb, is not as popular. For instance, how would you say 'good job' in Korean?

잘 했어.

(Jahl hae-ssuh.)

The literal meaning of the sentence is '(You) did well,' which is another way of saying '(You) did a good job.'

진짜 더워요.

(Jeen-jjah duh-wuh-yoh.)

더워 (duh-wuh) or 덥다 (duhb-ddah) means '(It's) hot.' So 진짜 덥다 (Jeen-jjah duhb-ddah) would mean it is a really hot day. 진짜 (jeen-jjah) can mean 'very' as well as 'really.'

많이 드세요.

(Mah-nee deu-seh-yoh.)

드세요 (deu-seh-yoh) is the JDM form of 먹다 (muhg-ddah), which means 'eat.' So 많이 드세요 (Mah-nee deu-seh-yoh) means 'Eat a lot' or 'Enjoy your meal.'

빨리 가자.

(Bbahl-lee gah-jah.)

가자 (gah-jah) is a form of 가다 (gah-dah). When a verb ends with -자 (-jah), it means 'let's (blank).' So 빨리 가자 (Bbahl-lee gah-jah) means 'Let's go fast' or 'Hurry up.'

사람이 굉장히 많네.

(Sah-rah-mee gwehng-jahng-hee mahn-neh.)

사람 (sah-rahm) is 'person.' 많네 (mahn-neh) is a form of 많다 (mahn-tah), which is an adjective verb.

It means there is 'a lot' of something. So this sentence is a way of saying 'There are a lot of people.'

31. Answering Adverbs

Q. How can I answer questions in Korean?

We have already talked about how some questions can be answered with a simple yes or no whereas some questions can not. Let's go through 'yes' and 'no' in Korean once more.

Yes: 어 (uh), 응 (eung), 네 (neh), 예 (yeah)

No: 아니 (ah-nee), 아니요 (ah-nee-yoh)

Which one of these words would you use to answer the following question?

한국 사람이에요?

(Hahn-goog ssah-rah-mee-eh-yoh?)

한국 (hahn-goog) is 'Korea' or 'South Korea' and 사람 (sah-rahm) is 'person.' So the question means 'Are you Korean?' The -요 (-yoh) at the end indicates this question is in JDM. So it is likely that the response should be in JDM as well. This means you only have three options; 네 (neh), 예 (yeah), and 아니요 (ah-nee-yoh). (Remember, 네 (neh) and 예 (yeah) both mean 'yes.') Here is a possible scenario.

A: 한국 사람이에요? (Hahn-goog ssah-rah-mee-eh-yoh?)

B: 네, 맞아요. (Neh, mah-jah-yoh.)

맞아요 (mah-jah-yoh) means '(that's) right.' But what if you are not Korean?

A: 한국 사람이에요? (Hahn-goog ssah-rah-mee-eh-yoh?)

B: 아니요, 중국 사람이에요. (Ah-nee-yoh, joong-goog ssah-rah-mee-eh-yoh.)

There are no subjects in both sentences. But we can still guess the subject for A is 'you' whereas the subject for B is 'I.' 중국 사람 (joong-goog ssah-rahm) means 'Chinese person,' so the response means 'No, I'm Chinese.'

Q. What about questions that start with 'what,' 'who,' 'when,' etc.?

If a question starts with a word like 'how,' then you must answer it in your own words. Here is one example.

여기 화장실이 어디에요?

(Yuh-ghee hwah-jahng-shee-ree uh-dee-eh-yoh?)

여기 (yuh-ghee) means 'here' or 'around here.' 화장실 (hwah-jahng-sheel) is 'bathroom.' -이 (-ee) is attached at the end, showing this noun is the subject. 어디에요 (uh-dee-eh-yoh) is 'where' as a question in JDM. Here are a couple of ways one might respond.

A

저기로 가시면 돼요.

(Juh-ghee-roh gah-shee-myuhn dwae-yoh.)

B

잘 모르겠어요.

(Jahl moh-reu-geh-ssuh-yoh.)

A says 'It's over there,' which implies that the speaker is pointing toward a direction. B, on the other hand, means 'I don't know' or 'I'm not sure.'

32. More Suffixes

Q. What do -과 (-gwah) and -와 (-wah) mean?

They are conjunction suffixes, meaning 'and.' Let's see how we can say 'Tom and Jerry' in Korean. By the way, 'Tom' is 톰 (tohm) and 'Jerry' is 제리 (jeh-ree).

톰과 제리

(tohm-gwah jeh-ree)

Because 톰 (tohm) ends with a closed sound, -과 (-gwah) was used. But what about 'Jerry and Tom?'

제리와 톰

(jeh-ree-wah tohm)

Since 제리 (jeh-ree) ends with an open sound, -와 (-wah) is attached to the noun and not -과 (-gwah). Let's try one more. Try to guess what the following might mean.

노인과 바다

(noh-een-gwah bah-dah)

You may not recognize the words, but did you spot -과 (-gwah) in the middle? Of course, the letter 과 (gwah) could be just a part of a word, as in 사과 (sah-gwah). But it is more likely that 노인과 바다 (noh-een-gwah bah-dah) probably means 'A and B.' 노인 (noh-een) means 'old person' and 바다 (bah-dah) means 'sea' or 'ocean.' So 노인과 바다 (noh-een-gwah bah-dah) refers to 'The Old Man and the Sea,' a book written by Ernest Hemingway. But what if Hemingway titled the book 'The Sea and the Old Man' instead?

바다와 노인

(bah-dah-wah noh-een)

Once again, the suffix is changed to -와 (-wah) because 바다 (bah-dah) ends with a vowel sound.

Q. What about -으로 (eu-roh) and -로 (roh)?

Both -으로 (eu-roh) and -로 (-roh) have two different meanings. One meaning is 'to' or 'toward.' For example, 'to New York' in Korean is 뉴욕으로 (nyou-yoh-geu-roh). 'To Malaysia' is 말레이시아로 (mahl-leh-ee-shee-ah-roh).

Another meaning is 'with' or 'by.' Let's take a look at the following sentence.

비행기로 왔어요.

(Bee-haeng-ghee-roh wah-ssuh-yoh.)

Even if you do not know the words, you might be able to guess that 비행기 (bee-haeng-ghee) is the subject and 왔어요 (wah-ssuh-yoh) is the main verb. 비행기 (bee-haeng-ghee) means 'airplane' and 왔어요 (wah-ssuh-yoh) means 'came' or 'arrived.' So what does the sentence mean in English?

(I) came by airplane.

So -으로/-로 (-eu-roh/-roh) works as a preposition (or postposition) whereas -과/-와 (-gwah/-wah) works as a conjunction. This is why knowing basic suffixes is very important. (Fortunately, for beginners, spoken Korean often neglects them unlike written Korean.)

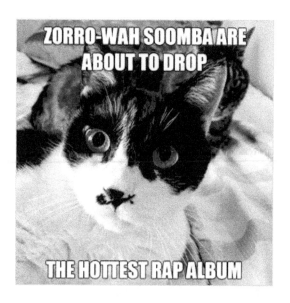

33. Time in Korean

Q. How do I tell time in Korean?

Telling time in Korean is pretty straight forward. As long as you are familiar with the number words between one and sixty, it should not be too difficult. But before we get to the numbers, let's see what the units of time are in Korean.

Hour: 시 (shee), 시간 (shee-gahn)

Minute: 분 (boon)

Second: 초 (choh)

When you want to talk about a specific hour, say the seventh hour, use 시 (shee). For talking about the amount of hours or 'time,' use 시간 (shee-gahn) instead. (No pluralization is needed for telling time.) Here is the list of all the hours on the clock.

1 o'clock: 한 시 (hahn shee)

2 o'clock: 두 시 (doo shee)

3 o'clock: 세 시 (seh shee)

4 o'clock: 네 시 (neh shee)

5 o'clock: 다섯 시 (dah-suht ssee)

6 o'clock: 여섯 시 (yuh-suht ssee)

7 o'clock: 일곱 시 (eel-gohb ssee)

8 o'clock: 여덟 시 (yuh-duhl ssee)

9 o'clock: 아홉 시 (ah-hohb ssee)

10 o'clock: 열 시 (yuhl ssee)

11 o'clock: 열한 시 (yuhl-hahn shee)

12 o'clock: 열두 시 (yuhl-doo shee)

Since these are fairly small numbers, the Korean-based words are used. For minutes and seconds, the Chinese-based words are used instead. Here are a few examples.

1 minute: 일 분 (eel boon)

5 minutes: 오 분 (oh boon)

10 minutes: 십 분 (sheeb bboon)

15 minutes: 십오 분 (shee-boh boon)

30 minutes: 삼십 분 (sahm-sheeb bboon)

45 minutes: 사십오 분 (sah-shee-boh boon)

60 minutes: 육십 분 (youg-sseeb bboon)

It is the same way with 초 (choh) or 'second.' Just replace the word 분 (boon) above with 초 (choh).

Now how about we make time more realistic?

8:50 a.m.

8:50 in the morning in Korean is **오전 여덟 시 오십 분** (oh-juh nyuh-duhl ssee oh-sheeb bboon). It is rather long, so let's break it down. **오전** (oh-juhn) means 'morning' or 'a.m.' Unlike in English, this word comes before the time and not after. **여덟** (yuh-duhl) is '8' and **시** (shee) is 'hour.' **오십** (oh-sheeb) is '50' and **분** (boon) is 'minute.' To make it easier, we can use English words for the numbers.

오전 8시 50분

(oh-juh neight-ssee fifty-boon)

So **오전** (oh-juhn) means 'a.m.' What about 'p.m.' in Korean?

1:05 p.m.

This is **오후 한 시 오 분** (oh-hoo hahn shee oh boon). You can probably guess that **오후** (oh-hoo) means 'p.m.' It can also be used to mean 'afternoon' or 'night' while discussing time.

4:20 p.m.

4:20 in the afternoon in Korean is **오후 네 시 이십 분** (oh-hoo neh-shee ee-sheeb bboon). Most of the time, it will be written as **오후 4시 20분**. So what do people do at 4:20 p.m. in South Korea? Well, they are not having too much fun (if you know what I mean).

7:30 p.m.

7:30 p.m. is **오후** 7시 30분 (oh-hoo eel-gohb-ssee sahm-sheeb-bboon). **삼십 분** (sahm-sheeb bboon) can be replaced with **반** (bahn), which means 'half.' So the expression can become **일곱 시 반** (eel-gohb ssee bahn) to mean 'seven and a half.' 2:30 is 2시 **반** (doo-shee bahn). 11:30 is 11시 **반** (yuhl-hahn-shee bahn).

Q. How can I say something like 'five hours' or 'two and a half hours' in Korean?

Sometimes, you need to tell the duration of time. How would say something will take five hours?

A

다섯 시

(dah-suht ssee)

B

다섯 시간

(dah-suht ssee-gahn)

A means the 'fifth hour' or 'five o'clock.' On the other hand, B says 'five hours' because of **시간** (shee-gahn). Let's look at another example.

A

두 시 반

(doo shee bahn)

B

두 시간 반

(doo shee-gahn bahn)

Once again, **반** (bahn) means 'half.' So A either shows the time of 2:30 a.m. or 2:30 p.m. whereas B says 'two and a half hours.'

Q. How do I say 'morning,' 'afternoon,' 'evening,' and 'night' in Korean?

Here are all the words associated with telling time.

Morning: **아침** (ah-cheem), **오전** (oh-juhn)

Noon: **점심** (juhm-sheem)

Afternoon: **오후** (oh-hoo)

Evening: **저녁** (juh-nyuhg)

Night: **밤** (bahm)

아침 (ah-cheem), 점심 (juhm-sheem), and 저녁 (juh-nyuhg) actually mean 'breakfast,' 'lunch,' and 'dinner,' respectively.

34. Dates in Korean

Q. How do I say the twelve months in Korean?

In English, a different word represents each month from January to December. However, in Korean, all you have to do is combine a number with 월 (wuhl).

January: 일월 (ee-rwuhl)

February: 이월 (ee-wuhl)

March: 삼월 (sah-mwuhl)

April: 사월 (sah-wuhl)

May: 오월 (oh-wuhl)

June: 유월 (you-wuhl)

July: 칠월 (cheel-wuhl)

August: 팔월 (pahl-wuhl)

September: 구월 (goo-wuhl)

October: 시월 (shee-wuhl)

November: 십일월 (shee-beel-wuhl)

December: 십이월 (shee-bee-wuhl)

월 (wuhl) means 'month' in Korean. So you get the month of the year by putting a number and this word together. It is pretty straight forward except there are a couple of minor exceptions. You may have already noticed how the word for 'June' is not written as 육월 (you-gwuhl). Also, 'October' in Korean is not written as 십월 (shee-bwuhl). (The pronunciations are slightly different because people developed a habit of pronouncing them differently over the years.)

Q. What about telling specific dates in Korean?

In East Asia, dates are given in the year-month-day order like the following.

YYYY-MM-DD

YY-MM-DD

So '07-05-19' means 'May 19th, 2007' and not 'July 5th, 2019.'

'Year' in Korean is 년 (nyuhn) and 'day' in Korean is 일 (eel). Here is what dates in Korean look like.

_____년 ____월 ____일

_____-nyuhn ____-wuhl ____-eel

For instance, 'May 19th, 2007' would be written as 2007년 5월 19일 (ee-chuhn-cheel-nyuh noh-wuhl sheeb-ggoo-eel).

35. Korean Proverbs

Q. What are some common sayings used by Korean speakers?

Now we are ready to see some actual sentences that people say. Proverbs are a great way to learn new words and sentence structures. You can also use them repeatedly in a variety of situations. So let's discuss ten popular proverbs almost any Korean speaker knows about.

1. 돌다리도 두들겨 보고 건너라 (dohl-dah-ree-doh doo-deul-gyuh boh-goh guhn-nuh-rah)

돌 (dohl) = stone, rock

다리 (dah-ree) = bridge

두들기다 (doo-deul-ghee-dah) = knock, tap

보다 (boh-dah) = try, attempt

건너다 (guhn-nuh-dah) = cross

돌다리 (dohl-dah-ree) means 'stone bridge' and is the subject noun. The suffix -도 (-doh) changes it to 'even a stone bridge.' -여/-겨 보고 (-yuh/-gyuh boh-goh) is used between two verbs to mean 'try A before B.' 건너다 (guhn-nuh-dah) is in form of 건너라 (guhn-nuh-rah) to show that it is a command or advice. So what does it mean all together?

Try knocking on even a stone bridge before you cross.

In other words, be careful no matter what. A bridge made of stone is most likely safe, but try to be careful nonetheless because accidents can happen at any time.

2. 말 안 하면 귀신도 모른다 (mah rahn hah-myuhn gwee-sheen-doh moh-reun-dah)

말 (mahl) = words, speaking

귀신 (gwee-sheen) = ghost

모른다 (moh-reun-dah) = do not know, would not know

We already discussed 안 (ahn), which means 'not.' 하다 (hah-dah), meaning 'do,' has changed to 하면 (hah-myuhn) to add the word 'if.' 귀신도 (gwee-sheen-doh) is 귀신 (gwee-sheen) and the suffix -도 (-doh), which makes it 'even a ghost.' Here is the complete the translation.

Even a ghost wouldn't know (how you feel) if you don't speak.

If you want people to know what you think or how you feel, then you must express yourself. If you don't, well, then even a ghost has no clue. (Actually, that may be a good thing.)

3. 작은 고추가 더 맵다 (jah-geun goh-choo-gah duh maeb-ddah)

작다 (jahg-ddah) = small

고추 (goh-choo) = chili pepper

더 (duh) = more

맵다 (maeb-ddah) = spicy, hot

When an adjective verb like 작다 (jahg-ddah) comes before a noun, its form changes. So 작은 고추 (jah-geun goh-choo) means 'small chili pepper.' 더 맵다 (duh maeb-ddah) is simply 'is more spicy.'

A small chili pepper is more spicy.

In other words, the smaller the chili pepper, the more spicy it is. This proverb teaches people to look down upon people with small figures.

4. 병 주고 약 준다 (byuhng joo-goh yahg jjoon-dah)

병 (byuhng) = illness, sickness

주다 (joo-dah) = give

약 (yahg) = medicine, pill, drug

주다 (joo-dah) plus 'and' is 주고 (joo-goh). 준다 (joon-dah) is a common way of using 주다 (joo-dah) in a sentence. So what does this proverb mean?

Give medicine after giving an illness.

It possesses a sarcastic tone to it. Let's say somebody has hurt you but tried to make up for it. Now you may have to forgive that person even though you don't feel like it.

5. 바늘 도둑이 소 도둑 된다 (bah-neul doh-doo-ghee soh doh-doog dwehn-dah)

바늘 (bah-neul) = needle

도둑 (doh-doog) = thief, buglar

소 (soh) = cow, cattle

되다 (dweh-dah) = be, become

This one is almost self-explanatory. Can you guess what it means?

A needle thief becomes a cow thief.

A long time ago, many people in Korea were farmers. For them, cows were huge assets. A needle, however, was worth much less. So what this proverb says is if you start getting into trouble at an early age, you are going to end up in bigger trouble later on. Stealing a needle may seem like a big deal at first, but once you develop a habit of doing it, you are likely to steal something much more valuable. So it is wise to not go in that direction in the first place.

6. 하나를 보면 열을 안다 (hah-nah-reul boh-myuh nyuh-reu rahn-dah)

알다 (ahl-dah) = know

보면 (boh-myuh) is a combination of 보다 (boh-dah) and -면 (-myuhn), which means 'if (you) see.' So what does it mean?

Sees one, knows ten.

This proverb works as a compliment given to a person who seems very bright. He is so bright when you teach him one, he understands ten.

7. **찬물도 위아래가 있다** (chahn-mool-doh wee-ah-rae-gah eet-ddah)

찬물 (chahn-mool) = cold water

위아래 (wee-ah-rae) = top and bottom, up and down

있다 (eet-ddah) = there is

Here is a direct translation.

Even cold water has top and bottom.

It doesn't make sense, does it? In South Korea, you don't get to eat or even grab a spoon before the oldest person at the table starts to eat. So if you are having dinner with your mom and dad, you wait for your parents to eat before you start eating. This is especially true if you are dining with somebody other than your parents like your grandparents. If you start eating before your grandpa or grandma takes a bite, your parents will scold you because it is considered offensive. OK. Back to the proverb. Water is not food or meal. But even water, even cold water has orders. So if you and your uncle want to drink some water, you must give the water to your uncle first. Then you can drink. That's what this proverb means, believe it or not.

8. 미운 놈 떡 하나 더 준다 (mee-woon nohm dduh kah-nah duh joon-dah)

밉다 (meeb-ddah) = not likeable, despicable

놈 (nohm) = boy, guy, jerk, bastard

떡 (dduhg) = rice cake

미운 놈 (mee-woon nohm) refers to a male person who is not likeable. 떡 하나 (dduh kah-nah) means 'one piece of rice cake.' 더 (duh) is 'more.' 준다 (joon-dah) is a form of 주다 (joo-dah), which means 'give.' So what does this proverb mean all together?

Give more rice cake to the despicable boy.

People sometimes pretend to be nice toward others, especially if they are not familiar with one another. So you might give the kid more food even if you don't like him.

9. 해가 서쪽에서 뜨겠다 (hae-gah suh-jjoh-geh-suh ddeu-geht-ddah)

해 (hae) = the Sun

서쪽 (suh-jjohg) = west

뜨다 (ddeu-dah) = rise, come up

서쪽에서 (suh-jjoh-geh-suh) means 'from the west.' 뜨겠다 (ddeu-geht-ddah) is a form of 뜨다 (ddeu-dah), meaning something could 'likely rise' or 'might rise.'

The Sun might rise from the west.

Of course, the Sun rises in the east. But when somebody does something strange, one might think the world is upside down. This proverb is sounds similar to 'Did you wake up on the wrong side of the bed?' However, it is usually used to show a pleasant or positive surprise in a sarcastic way.

10. 누워 떡 먹기 (noo-wuh dduhg muh-gghee)

눕다 (noob-ddah) = lie down

The word 떡 (dduhg) appears in many Korean proverbs because people in Korea consumed rice cake on a regular basis around the time these sayings were created. 먹기 (muh-gghee) is a gerund, turning the verb 'eat' into 'eating.' Can you guess what it means now? (It should be a piece of cake!)

Eating rice cake while lying down.

This means something is very easy to do. Of course, no one would actually eat rice cake while lying down; even though it is "easy as pie."

36. Sentence Translation

Q. Is there an easy way to translate Korean sentences into English?

Translating sentences between English and Korean is more of art than science. There is no exact way of doing it because every sentence has a different structure and meaning. Besides, English and Korean possess almost no similarities with each other. Luckily, there is a relatively easy way of converting English sentences into Korean sentences and vice versa. The method is known as Chop Chop Voila. (Because, why not?)

Here is a typical sentence in English.

I plan to go to Korea in a few months.

It has ten words, which are in different parts of speech. (For instance, 'few' is an adjective.) So what should be the first step of translating this sentence into Korean? First, we should locate the subject of the sentence. The subject can be seen as the head of a fish. It is not only very important but is also different from the body. So we should chop it off first. In this sentence, the subject is simply 'I.'

I / plan to go to Korea in a few months

The predicate, or the body, is the rest of the sentence. Now we make another chop right in the middle to split the body in half.

I / plan to go to Korea / in a few months

Now switch the positions of the two body parts.

I / in a few months / plan to go to Korea

We are already half way done. Now we split the two body parts once more.

I / in a / few months / plan to go / to Korea

Switch the positions again.

I / few months / in a / to Korea / plan to go

All we can just translate each word into Korean.

난 / 몇달 / 안에 / 한국에 / 갈 계획이다

(nahn / myuht-ddahl / ah-neh / hahn-goo-geh /

gahl gyeah-hweh-ghee-dah)

Let's remove the slashes and we are done.

난 몇달 안에 한국에 갈 계획이다.

(Nahn myuht-ddah rah-neh hahn-goo-geh

gahl gyeah-hweh-ghee-dah.)

Let's go through the steps one more time.

Original sentence:

1 2 3 4 5 6 7 8 9

I plan to go to Korea in a few months

1. Split the subject from the body:

1 / 2 3 4 5 6 7 8 9

I / plan to go to Korea in a few months

2. Split the body into two halves:

1 / 2 3 4 5 / 6 7 8 9

I / plan to go to Korea / in a few months

3. Switch the two body halves around:

1 / 6 7 8 9 / 2 3 4 5

I / in a few months / plan to go to Korea

4. Split the two body halves into four body halves:

1 / 6 7 / 8 9 / 2 3 / 4 5

I / in a / few months / plan to go / to Korea

5. Switch the positions of the split halves again:

1 / 8 9 / 6 7 / 4 5 / 2 3

I / few months / in a / to Korea / plan to go

6. Translate the words (and add suffixes if necessary):

난 / 몇달 / 안에 / 한국에 / 갈 계획이다

(nahn / myuht-ddahl / ah-neh / hahn-goo-geh / gahl gyeah-hweh-ghee-dah)

Because Korean is often spoken without a subject word, you may take out the subject if you wish. You can also change the ending of the main verb at the end from -**다** (-dah) to -**야** (-yah) to make it sound more conversational.

몇달 안에 한국에 갈 계획이야.

(Myuht-ddah rah-neh hahn-goo-geh

gahl gyeah-hweh-ghee-yah.)

How about one more translation?

Jihoon was happy to see Amy.

Remember the first step? Chop off the head of the fish. The subject is Jihoon and the rest is the body. Let's go through the same steps.

1. Split the subject from the body:

1 / 2 3 4 5 6 7 8 9

Jihoon / was happy to see Amy

2. Split the body into two halves:

1 / 2 3 4 5 / 6 7 8 9

Jihoon / was happy / to see Amy

3. Switch the two body halves around:

1 / 6 7 8 9 / 2 3 4 5

Jihoon / to see Amy / was happy

4. Split the two body halves into four body halves:

1 / 6 7 / 8 9 / 2 3 / 4 5

Jihoon / to see / Amy / was / happy

5. Switch the positions of the split halves again:

1 / 8 9 / 6 7 / 4 5 / 2 3

Jihoon / Amy / to see / happy / was

6. Translate the words (and add suffixes if necessary):

지훈은 / 에이미를 / 봐서 / 행복 / 했다

(jee-hoo-neun / eh-ee-mee-reul / bwah-suh / haeng-bohg / haet-ddah)

지훈은 에이미를 봐서 행복했다.

(Jee-hoo-neu neh-ee-mee-reul

bwah-suh haeng-boh-kaet-ddah.)

Notice how 'Jihoon' was translated as 지훈은 (jee-hoo-neun) and not 지훈 (jee-hoon). Similarly, 'Amy' became 에이미를 (eh-ee-mee-reul) and not 에이미 (eh-ee-mee). When you have the subject and one or more objects placed right next to each other, it is usually a good practice to add suffixes to avoid confusion.

Q. Does Chop Chop Voila work with every sentence?

Unfortunately, Chop Chop Voila has its flaws. Because there are many different sentence structures, CCV only works some of the time. What is important is that it gives you a general idea of how sentences can be translated so you can improvise. Let's take a look at a sentence where Chop Chop Voila may not work as well as the previous examples.

After this month, Jane will return to her previous school.

This sentence does not start with the subject, which is 'Jane.' So we must take out 'after this month' and put it back in at the end.

Jane will return to her previous school.

Now we can chop the subject from the body.

Jane / will return to her previous school

Now we split the body in half and switch them around.

Jane / her previous school / will return to

Now we are supposed to make another chop chop within the body parts. But 'her previous school' should not change since it follows the same word order in Korean. On the other hand, 'will return to' can be divided into 'will' and 'return to' and then switched to 'return to' and 'will.' So we have the following.

Jane / her previous school / return to / will

We are ready to translate the words into Korean and add suffixes to 제인 (jeh-een) and 학교 (hahg-ggyoh).

제인은 / 그녀의 예전 학교로 / 돌아갈 것이다

(jeh-ee-neun / geu-nyuh-eui yeah-juhn

hahg-ggyoh-roh / doh-rah-gahl gguh-shee dah)

Now it is time to put back 'after this month' or 이번 달 후에 (ee-buhn ddahl hoo-eh).

이번 달 후에 / 제인은 / 그녀의 예전 학교로 / 돌아갈 것이다

(ee-buhn ddahl hoo-eh / jeh-ee-neun /

geu-nyuh-eui yeah-juhn hahg-ggyoh-roh /

doh-rah-gahl gguh-shee-dah)

Remove the slashes and now the translation is complete.

이번 달 후에 제인은 그녀의 예전 학교로 돌아갈 것이다.

(Ee-buhn ddahl hoo-eh jeh-ee-neun

geu-nyuh-eui yeah-juhn hahg-ggyoh-roh

doh-rah-gahl gguh-shee-dah.)

Here is the translation of the original sentence by Google Translate.

이번 달 후에 Jane은 이전 학교로 돌아갈 것입니다.

Everything is essentially the same except the verb is in JDM and not BM.

Q. Does Chop Chop Voila work the other way?

Translating Korean sentences works the same way. Here is a sentence in Korean.

내일 전화기를 바꿀 거야.

(Nae-eel juhn-hwah-ghee-reul bah-ggool gguh-yah.)

The first thing we should do is to figure out if this sentence has the subject or not. The first word is 내일 (nae-eel), which does not seem to have a suffix. However, 전화기 (juhn-hwah-ghee) has -를 (-reul) attached at the end. That would mean this word is an object noun. So is 내일 (nae-eel) the subject? The answer is no. It is missing a subject suffix and the word means 'tomorrow,' which is usually used as an adverb. So what is the subject? It is likely 'I' or 나 (nah), which is implied. That means we have to insert it in the sentence since English sentences do require the subject to be explicit. Then we can take out all the suffixes to make translation easier.

Original sentence:

내일 전화기를 바꿀 거야. (Nae-eel juhn-hwah-ghee-reul bah-ggool gguh-yah.)

Insert the subject:

나는 내일 전화기를 바꿀 거야. (Nah-neun nae-eel juhn-hwah-ghee-reul bah-ggool gguh-yah.)

Remove suffixes:

나 내일 전화기 바꿀 거야. (Nah nae-eel juhn-hwah-ghee bah-ggool gguh-yah.)

Now we can follow the same steps as before.

1. Split the subject from the body:

나 / 내일 전화기 바꿀 거야

(nah / nae-eel juhn-hwah-ghee bah-ggool gguh-yah)

2. Split the body into two halves:

나 / 내일 전화기 / 바꿀 거야

(nah / nae-eel juhn-hwah-ghee / bah-ggool gguh-yah)

3. Switch the two body halves around:

나 / 바꿀 거야 / 내일 전화기

(nah / bah-ggool gguh-yah / nae-eel juhn-hwah-ghee)

4. Split the two body halves into four body halves:

나 / 바꿀 / 거야 / 내일 / 전화기

(nah / bah-ggool / guh-yah / nae-eel / juhn-hwah-ghee)

5. Switch the positions of the split halves again:

나 / 거야 / 바꿀 / 전화기 / 내일

(nah / guh-yah / bah-ggool / juhn-hwah-ghee / nae-eel)

6. Translate the words:

I / will / change / phone / tomorrow

Put the words together and voila!

I will change (my) phone tomorrow.

Pretty neat, eh? Unfortunately, Chop Chop Voila is not very effective during conversations. It is more for academic purposes. (For real-time translation, I'm sure there is an app for that.)

Hangul Pronunciations

Hangul Consonants

ㄱ = g/k   ㄴ = n   ㄷ = d   ㄹ = l/r   ㅁ = m

ㅂ = b   ㅅ = s/sh   ㅇ = o   ㅈ = j   ㅊ = ch

ㅋ = k   ㅌ = t   ㅍ = p   ㅎ = h   ㄲ = gg/kk

ㄸ = dd/tt   ㅃ = bb   ㅆ = ss   ㅉ = jj

Hangul Vowels

ㅏ = ah   ㅑ = yah   ㅓ = uh   ㅕ = yuh

ㅗ = oh   ㅛ = yoh   ㅜ = woo   ㅠ = you

ㅐ = ae   ㅒ = yaeh   ㅔ = eh   ㅖ = yeah

ㅘ = wah   ㅙ = wae   ㅚ = weh

ㅝ = wuh   ㅞ = weah   ㅟ = wee

ㅡ = eu   ㅣ = yee   ㅢ = eui

More Books

Korean Phrases with Cat Memes

500+ Korean phrases for travelers and beginners

400+ example sentences in English and Hangul

Cat memes of Soomba and Zorro

Available in eBook and paperback formats

Korean Words with Cat Memes (1 ~ 5)

250+ essential words (per book) for beginners

Example sentences in English and Hangul

Cat memes of Soomba and Zorro

Available in eBook and paperback formats

More Information

EASY KOREAN

Visit www.easy-korean.com for free Korean lessons, dictionary, and more.

EASY KOREAN on YouTube

Access grammar, listening, vocabulary, and hangul videos for beginners.

EASY KOREAN on Twitter (@EASY_KOREAN)

Follow EASY KOREAN on Twitter and get the latest updates.

9KOREA - Get Korea in English

Visit www.9korea.com for articles and more on living in Korea.

About the Author

Min Kim is the creator of EASY KOREAN among other projects. He was born in South Korea but spent his teenage years in the United States. He currently lives in Seoul with his two cats, Soomba and Zorro.

If you found this book helpful, please leave a review on the place of purchase. Thank you.

M.K.

CPSIA information can be obtained
at www.ICGtesting.com
Printed in the USA
BVHW010916190620
581843BV00014B/60

9 781978 091627